The *four* Passages of the HEART

Moving from Pain into Love

365 Daily Illuminations
to Transform Your Life

SARA WISEMAN

CONTENTS

Dedication

THE SEEKING OF CONSCIOUSNESS, the opening into love has no age, no gender, no country. For all of you who find this book, in the many mysterious and miraculous ways this may happen … welcome. It is written for and dedicated to you.

In earth life, in the human experience, the heart is the way in which we grow. We grow by opening our closed hearts up to ourselves, to one another, and finally, to the deepest, most profound aspect of the Divine. This is how we become One.

INTRODUCTION

There is a secret to living an extraordinary life—and it is a secret anyone may possess.

The secret isn't about attitude, intention, or the power of positive thinking. It's not about the Law of Attraction, The Secret, co-creation, or any of the current manifesting systems du jour. Nor is it about aligning with a particular teacher, belief system, or manifesto. Instead, it's about moving from the perception of pain into the reality of love.

Moving from pain into love.

This sounds so simple—too simple, in fact.

And yet, this journey is the true hero's quest of our lives.

It involves exposing the deepest, most guarded places inside of yourself.

It involves unearthing your most vulnerable, tender emotions.

It involves truly seeing what you have created in your life, without resistance, shame, or ego.

And most importantly, it involves cracking open your heart.

Not once.

But four times.

Now, no one is required to journey this path. Indeed, you may have worked hard to avoid this path entirely—by keeping your heart armored, sealed away, and numb to everything so you don't have to feel the pain.

That is one way to live.

But there is another way that allows you to move progressively from pain into love. In its simplest form, it involves bathing your heart in the light of Divine consciousness—which is, of course, where everything begins to change.

In this book you will find 365 Daily Illuminations that will guide you each day for an entire year, through the process of cracking open your heart—a process that will most assuredly bring about awareness, healing, and a consciousness shift.

You don't have to know anything special to begin this journey. You may have studied with masters, or done no spiritual work at all. You may have spent years in therapy, or never had a single session. You may have a strong belief system, or you may have lived your life without one. You may have had countless mystic experiences, or never a one.

It doesn't matter.

Simply start where you are, and take it day by day.

The transformation that happens during this year-long process will begin immediately. Even after a few days of reading the illuminations, you may notice changes happening in your life that may appear nothing short of miraculous.

Be assured, these so-called miracles aren't anything out of the ordinary. Instead, they're simply what happens when you allow your heart to open again, and yet again, into the radiant illumination of the Divine.

PART ONE

Moving from Pain into Love

CHAPTER ONE

The Four Passages

 The process of soul growth takes place neither in the body nor the mind, regardless of the practices, actions or achievements of a person during his or her lifetime. Instead, the only way to achieve soul growth as a human in this lifetime is through the progressive opening of the heart into four consecutive passages: pain, compassion, connection, and love.

My own heart first began to open in 2000, and it was not a pretty sight.

After decades of keeping the lid on a life overflowing with the incessant demands of family and work, the Universe decided to step in and—ahem—shift things.

If you've ever been in the midst of a cosmic intervention, you know the drill: everything happens at once, and all of it is impossibly difficult.

My case was no different.

Out of nowhere, my tidy little life began to implode as I experienced one tragic event after another. These included, but were not limited to a) a near death experience that left me with PTSD and the inability to travel or even drive without debilitating anxiety; b) the death of my father; and c) the slow unraveling of my marriage, which would end in divorce a few years later.

The pain was unbearable, and even as the storm clouds rumbled and lighting crackled on the horizon, I threw myself frantically into the distractions of daily life, in hopes that by pulling the proverbial covers over my head I could somehow ride out the storm.

However, escape was not my destiny.

I was destined to bottom out.

I was destined to know profound pain.

I was destined to be cracked open.

One night, during one of the lowest points in my life, I woke up alone into an eerie mid-dawn stillness and saw a vision in my bedroom. Looking back, it's hard to determine if what I saw was a dream, a Divine communication, or a state of sweet subconscious— I'm still not sure.

But what I saw clearly was this: a rusted tin box containing a heart so dark and shriveled, it was nearly unrecognizable. And as I peered into the hazy darkness, trying to see this image more clearly, I knew:

This was my heart.

Yet even as I stared in revulsion at this disturbing image, I saw it was beginning to change. It was opening, and inside I glimpsed something I had not yet heard about, something I would only learn the term for much later—a tiny, glowing jewel of a heart, radiant with light, the *Ananda Khanda*, as it is sometimes called in Sanskirt: the high heart, the spiritual heart, the heart within the heart.

I did not have a name or word for what it was, and yet I knew it in that moment.

In that instant of recognition the tin box began to crack away, and in my chest I felt an energetic opening: a heave, a shuddering, a slamming of impact to my heart. A sliver of light slanted in, and I gasped in wonder as my own inner heart, the heart within my heart, began to expand.

To be alone in the dark and feel your heart move inside your chest, even as your pulse races and the hair on your arms and the back of your neck stands up—to feel this coursing of energy you do not recognize as your own, even as you understand that something extraordinary and enthralling is happening to you. This is a profound experience.

As I sat, I felt my heart expand beyond the confines of the tin box, expanding until my wildly beating, fully human heart was extended to its fullest capacity, extending outside of my chest in pure love. I felt healing course through my body as rapid infusions of Divine light.

Now ... I wish I could say this particular Divine healing changed my life in a moment—that the next day I awakened as a fully conscious and loving being, One with All, with all of my earthly problems solved once and forever.

I did not.

I woke up as myself—a more tender self, perhaps; a self that had been opened, perhaps, but was still replete with all my faults and fears.

And yet ... this vision was a precursor of what would soon to arrive in my life. Within days, it became clear that I had embarked upon a much longer, more challenging journey of heart's opening—a journey I still travel each day.

For during this amazing experience, and as I began receiving spiritual teachings much later during meditation, I began to understand there are four passages—four openings—our hearts must move through. If we are to move from the prison of pain into a place where we can live wholly authentic, awakened, and loving lives, this is the only path we can take.

THE FOUR PASSAGES

What do we mean when we talk about the four passages of the heart? What do we mean when we talk about heart's opening?

Obviously, we're not talking about a physical opening in the heart: the heart's opening is energetic, just as all things are energetic.

We aren't talking about a one-time event, either. Instead, it's a progressive opening, a series of passages from one state of consciousness to another. Again, it doesn't happen all at once—that would be too much, too fast; a shock to the system. Instead, our hearts open slowly, when we are ready. We move through each passage as part of our soul growth, in Divine time.

Some folks bust their hearts open at a young age, determined from the get-go to live life at full throttle—to accept what life brings without hesitation, and to live their days in love and light regardless of situation.

This is a great way to live!

Others of us take longer, opening our hearts slowly as we move through our lessons of soul growth, as our experiences on earth teach us the lessons of wisdom, patience, humility.

Still others stay stuck for years, even decades, entombed in anger, sadness, and shame.

You will find yourself in one of these places now.

Right now, your heart is either fully open, partly open, or mostly shut.

If your heart is fully open, congratulations. Please give this book to a friend!

If your heart is partly open, this book will help you open it further.

If your heart is mostly shut, you may feel vulnerable as you read this book and consider what may happen—and how things might change— if you dare open your heart to the light.

FOUR SEQUENTIAL STAGES

The heart does not open at random. Instead, it opens in four sequential stages, each expansion building on the next. These four passages are...

* Heart of pain,
* Heart of compassion,
* Heart of connection,
* Heart of love.

Depending on where you find yourself on your personal journey of soul growth, you are in the midst of, or embarking upon, one of these passages right now. Let's take a look at what each passage means, and how it might show up in your life:

* If you are in *heart of pain*, the first passage, you are becoming aware; you're becoming a conscious person. This is a good thing! But in this first stage, you're examining your own unhappiness, anxiety, fear, rage, or guilt. For the first time, you are considering the idea of facing pain directly rather than avoiding it, numbing out, or blaming others for your misery.

For most people, heart of pain is the most difficult passage. Entering this passage signifies the clear desire to change your life from the inside out, and to become awake after years or decades of living life asleep.

* If you are in *heart of compassion*, the second passage, you have moved completely through pain and are ready to hold compassion for others and for yourself.

This doesn't mean you never feel pain again. It means you have a new way to think about pain, as something universal to the human condition. This passage allows you to understand that we are all, at our core, the same. We are Divine beings in human bodies, facing human challenges. At this stage you are becoming more conscious

* If you are in *heart of connection*, the third passage, you have become conscious. You have expanded your awareness to a level in which you recognize yourself as one of One. You see yourself first as a spiritual being. Earthly concerns fade as you connect yourself to the Oneness that surrounds us and *is* us. Spiritual and/or intuitive awakening are the hallmarks of this passage.

* If you are in *heart of love*, the fourth passage, you will be in a state of nirvana, bliss, true healing, fulfillment, peace and happiness—if not all the time, then most of the time. This is the state of *Ananda Khanda*, loosely translated as the high heart, the spiritual heart. It is the opening of the deepest heart within all your hearts; the innermost heart under all of your layers, armor, resistance, and distractions, into the state of pure love.

It is a state of transcendence, and of transmutation into grace.

In this fourth passage, in this state of pure love, you are fully conscious; the most conscious a human can be. Nothing is withheld. You are conscious of everything, in all moments.

Many of us can access these higher states some of the time; we can go to this state momentarily, or even longer. Yet in true heart of connection you live there all the time, in every moment of your existence. At this point in time few people on earth have the ability to remain in this passage all the time—only the saints, the holy ones, the ascended masters.

Thus, as your consciousness expands, you might expect to learn how to experience heart of love—but the ability to stay there may be the task of this and future lifetimes.

HOW TO USE THIS BOOK

The first part of this book offers a simple overview of each of the four passages, so you can determine where you are now on your path. For example, if you are beginning in heart of pain, which is the place most of us begin, you'll find it useful to know what to expect: how you might feel, what you might experience, what may happen as you open to that passage.

When you move to heart of compassion, you need to know how that might feel, and so on. Thus, these initial chapters are meant to guide you from wherever you are.

However, the essence of this book is found within the 365 Daily Illuminations. Your awareness will truly begin to expand as you begin working with these teachings. Each day you will want to read an illumination and answer the questions that follow in writing, or in quiet contemplation. Take as much the time you need—this may be ten minutes for some, an hour for others.

While the illuminations may at first seem simple, they are a type of koan for the mind, designed to lead you deeper into conscious awakening. As you work through each illumination, people, events, experiences, memories, and emotions may flood your awareness. This is a normal part of the process of releasing and healing.

Be patient with yourself as you move through this practice.

As humans, it takes time for us to learn and grow. If you were to blast through all the four passages of the heart—from pain, into compassion, into connection, into love—all at once, you'd have problems integrating this experience. It sometimes happens to people in this way, but the rush of energy is very difficult for our emotional selves to deal with.

Thus, be patient with yourself. Use the illuminations as a daily spiritual practice, and have confidence that your understanding will unfold with correct timing; that there is no hurry or concern for the pace of your awakening.

Simply begin, and trust in the journey.

CHAPTER TWO

The First Passage

HEART OF PAIN

 The human heart can hold everything. The Divine soul is both everything and beyond everything. Allowing this first passage, descending down and into pain, is what allows you to understand your full being, both human and Divine.

Meg came to me with a deeply wounded heart. Just two months earlier her beloved husband had died unexpectedly of a heart attack. Meg was only 42, but she'd been married for 20 years—they had a wonderful relationship that spanned decades.

Now she was trying to pick up the pieces.

Initially, I was taken aback by Meg's calm demeanor and the matter-of-fact way she talked about her husband's cremation, funeral service, and other details. I expected her to cry when she spoke about him or show other signs of grief, but to my surprise, she was dry-eyed as she sat in my office.

As we talked, the situation became clear. Meg confessed she hadn't been able to do much besides the basics, not even getting rid of her late husband's clothing and personal affects.

"His bathrobe is still hanging where it always hung and his toothbrush is still in the cup by the bathroom sink," she said with something akin to pride.

"Almost as if he still lives there?" I asked gently.

"Oh, he still lives there!" she agreed readily. "He's always in the house; I talk to him all the time." And then, more hesitantly, "Is it okay for me to still be seeing him?"

I assured her that at this point in her grieving, seeing him was completely normal.

"Grieving!" she shook her head angrily. "I don't need to grieve! I'm not a crier, for one thing. And he was an upbeat guy—he wouldn't want me to be sad."

Rockets of understanding went off in my head, as I realized Meg was not dry-eyed because she was heartless or unfeeling. Meg was dry-eyed because she had not yet allowed herself to recognize her pain.

She was still numb, armored, unreleased.

As I looked energetically into the situation, I saw something else—that Meg was afraid if she allowed herself to feel the pain of her husband's death *it would be too much to bear.*

I didn't say anything right away, but instead had her close her eyes and breathe deeply until she was relaxed. I then guided her into a light trance, in hopes the Divine would bring healing. Within moments, I noticed an energetic presence arriving into the room: it was her departed husband in spirit form, wearing his signature work jacket, flannel shirt, jeans, and leather work gloves. As I waited to hear whatever message he might have for his wife, I noticed with surprise that he was crying.

Now, I've seen a lot of people cry—I sometimes joke that half my office budget is allocated for Kleenex—but I've never seen anyone cry like this. He filled the room with heart rendering, uncontrollable sobs, and he held out his etheric arms to Meg, gasping "I didn't mean to leave. I never wanted to go."

He wasn't crying for himself—the departed are usually fairly serene once they get to other side. Instead, he was crying for her.

As he cried, she sat stiffly, as if she didn't believe what was happening. Yet even though she remained impassive, my own body responded—I felt a sudden flooding in my heart, and I too began to cry, acting as a full conduit for his emotions. His anguish was coming through my physical body, and I sobbed with those deep, painful tears that hurt your eyes and clog your head and never seem to stop, repeating his message to my client.

I didn't mean to leave.

I never wanted to go.

Trying to get hold of myself—for I literally could not stop crying—I looked further into the situation and saw that my client's heart was energetically swaddled, like the bandaging on ancient mummies—and underneath these layers and mufflers and paddings of emotional wrapping, her heart beat black with pain.

"Your grieving will start next week," I gasped, barely able to get the words out. "What I'm feeling now—you're going to feel soon."

Sure enough, the next week Meg called to cancel our appointment, saying she was incapacitated with sorrow. After months of trying to hold everything together her heart had ruptured with pain—and with this agonizing release she felt everything she'd been resisting for so long. It took her husband, in spirit form, to show her by his own tears (and mine) that it was time for her to let go.

The time was right for her to open into heart of pain—the first passage.

At our next session Meg was visibly sad, but calm. "I cried for two weeks solid," she said. "And I haven't stopped; I'm still crying—it comes on like waves."

Interestingly, she said that her fear of pain was actually worse than the pain itself. "When I finally let myself cry, something shifted. I'd been so scared that I wouldn't be able to survive the pain, but when I finally let go, something released."

For Meg, anticipating the pain was the worst part of grieving. When she finally allowed herself to open into heart of pain she experienced an energetic shift that was initially painful—but was the beginning of a profound healing.

THE HEART'S ARMOR

So often, we think of our heart as a brilliant jewel that must be placed in a velvet case and locked away in the strongest vault. We armor up to protect this radiant jewel, like warriors who add layer upon layer of chain mail and steel before going into battle.

We lock up our hearts and throw away the keys; we hide our hearts in hidden crevices at the back of the darkest caves; we stuff them into tiny metal boxes so they can never be exposed again. We imagine that if we can just protect and pad and armor our hearts, we will never know pain again.

But of course this not true.

Part of being human is to understand that pain exists—not just as physical pain, but as emotional pain. We may feel emotional pain that stems from:

◆ Betrayal	◆ Violence
◆ Loss	◆ Poverty
◆ Sadness	◆ Illness
◆ Depression	◆ Addiction
◆ Fear	◆ Abuse
◆ Anxiety	◆ Tragedy
◆ Hatred	◆ Disaster
◆ Stress	◆ Violence
◆ Toxicity	◆ Grief
◆ Imbalance	

Even for those who are committed to positive thinking—those who follow such upbeat modern manifestos as the Law of Attraction or The Secret; those who live in light and love; those who receive Divine guidance regularly; those who are committed to raising their vibration on this planet—even these folks have at one time or another in their lives experienced feelings of pain, fear, shame, remorse, grief, and sadness.

The Universe is always in flux. We exist in a continuum of sorrow and happiness, destruction, and creation, pain and joy.

There is no way to change this, as far as I know.

But, as beings who are here for soul growth; as beings who have come to this earth to learn soul lessons, to expand our consciousness, and to move forward in the Divine, there is one way to move forward from the abyss.

It is to open our hearts.

This simple, everyday act has the power to transform everything.

 When you have moved into the first passage of pain, you will see pain everywhere. This is a temporary state. You will see pain in all beings who are distracted and numb, and you will see pain in all beings who are in the pain state. Recognizing you are not alone, you are not different or separate, and that pain is Universal before a first opening, is a lesson in soul growth.

For Meg after she lost her husband, the first step for her was to move from numbness to the experience of opening into pain.

This wasn't pleasant or easy for Meg.

But when she finally allowed herself to let pain wash over her like a rushing wave, she was immediately transformed. Upon illumination, the pain dissipated. And when her grieving eventually subsided, a process that initially hit hard for several months and then continued for two more years, Meg was left with something new: calm, peace, and healing. By the time the pain was through, Meg had moved into the next state of consciousness—that of compassion—for herself, for her situation, and for her departed husband.

This took a long time.

She could not jump into compassion simply because she wanted to be there, or because it sounded like a better place to be.

Meg—like all of us—needed to start where she found herself. In this case, in my office, absolutely numb with grief, with her husband appearing as a spirit who showed her through his own tears the great sadness she held within.

Thus, the first step on Meg's journey was her initial release into heart of pain.

Without this first step, she would have remained stuck: dry-eyed and numb, afraid of facing her fear—for months, years, maybe even the rest of her life

But because her husband, wise and loving even after death, came back to show her the pain that filled her own heart, she was able to look at it. She could enter into it and finally, over time, she could surrender into it and move into a new passage of healing, a new state of conscious awareness.

What happened to Meg is a miracle available to us all.

For Meg's heart, even in the midst of its profound and unbearable pain, did not crack asunder.

Instead, like a flower, it opened into the light.

THE CHOICE IS YOURS

As you exist on this earth, chances are good that your heart will feel pain. It might be something as tragic as the death of a loved one, as Meg experienced.

Or, it might be something a lot smaller—maybe even something insignificant: a harsh word from a family member, a perceived snub from a friend—something so small as to be almost inconsequential.

Whatever happens, it's a given that at some time in your life, you're going to face pain. This isn't about whether you have pain or not. Instead...

* It's what you do with the pain that matters.

* It's how you process emotion in your heart.

* It's about your willingness to move through this first passage, into the compassion that awaits.

Now, no one is saying you have to choose to open your heart. You don't. No law, earthly or Divine, says you have to open your heart during this lifetime. You can stay stuck for as long as you want— even your whole life.

You can distract yourself with all sorts of achievements and goals and "to dos." You can tuck your heart away in a tin box. You can armor it with pads and protection. You can hide it away in a deep, dark place. You can cover it with clouds of depression. You can surround it with rage and blame. You can numb out with every kind of addiction and misery.

All these are methods most of us have used at one time or another.

But after a certain point ... after enough years of avoidance and distraction and simply hitting our heads against the wall, most of us come to realize there has to be another way.

A path in which you allow yourself to face that initial passage of pain and to open, progressively and steadily, into new and higher ranges of consciousness.

Perhaps we cannot easily attain the bliss of the final, fourth passage of heart of love right away, but surely we can approach this state of love regularly and often. We can touch base with it; we can infuse ourselves with it; we can spread it over ourselves like a healing balm.

And absolutely, without doubt, we can open our hearts to the second and third passages of sequential consciousness: from pain to compassion to connection.

We can allow our hearts to open into these passages slowly, over time, as we move through our lives. Or we can take a great leap and allow all four of the passages to happen all at once, such as might occur in a spiritual awakening.

Timing isn't important.

What's most important is that we begin. The sheer act of illuminating what is dark, of looking deeply at what we feel, of recognizing and acknowledging that even though we have tried to lock our hearts away, the pain is there—this illumination alone allows the transition to start.

ENTERING THE PASSAGE

The first passage through heart of pain is the most difficult.

It's the passage that takes the most courage, the most chutzpah. Even if you have friends or family standing in the wings to support you in your process, it remains a private journey, an emotional hero's quest—it is something you must do alone.

You may recognize you're ready to enter the passage of pain if you experience the following:

+ You feel bored, ill at ease, and nothing seems interesting or fun.
+ Your relationships are continually in conflict; you can't seem to reach a place of harmony with others.
+ You have financial woes you can't seem to resolve.
+ Your primary relationships aren't healthy and you don't know how to fix them.
+ You feel trapped in a relationship or marriage because of money, kids, tradition, or culture.
+ Your relationships with key people in your life—mother, father, siblings, partner, children—are distant.
+ You have the feeling there's no way for these relationships to be patched or saved.
+ You don't like your job.

- You don't like where you live.
- You wake up feeling angry, stressed, anxious, or sad.
- You don't have a clear picture of where you're headed in life.
- You numb yourself out in the pursuit of money, material items, achievement, experiences, and future spinning.
- You numb yourself out with drugs, alcohol, cigarettes, food, the computer, a smart phone, pornography, sex, and other addictions.
- You were abused (sexually, physically or emotionally) as a child.
- Your sexual orientation is rejected by your family, social group, or culture.
- You feel religion has abandoned you.
- You have trouble meditating, praying, or trusting the Divine.
- You feel God/One/All/Universe has abandoned you.
- You feel karma is not on your side.
- You don't feel you're living the life you were born to have.
- You feel stuck.
- You feel numb.
- You want so much more, but you don't know how to get there.

This is a rather long list, and not a pleasant one. Take a look and decide which aspects of the list apply to you. If more than a few items resonate, or if you have an emotional reaction to anything on the list, simply allow yourself to understand this.

Often, we resist recognizing how deeply we are in pain.

Often, we resist recognizing how deeply we are stuck.

Take a look and decide where you are and if this is your situation now.

ALLOWING PAIN

The only way to move through pain and move through the passage of heart of pain is to acknowledge you are in pain, and to ask for Divine help.

If you have been numb to your pain, if you've armored your heart, if you've distracted yourself with a million things in your life— even now, upon reading this, you may be resist the reality of pain by saying something like...

+ I have no pain, my life is as good as you could expect,

+ I don't have time to focus on pain, I'm too busy,

+ What's done is done. Why look back? You can't change the past,

...then you have not yet moved through heart of pain.

When you become fully integrated as a person who has moved into a higher state of consciousness, you'll recognize the existence of pain in your life as a normal part of the human experience. You will not welcome pain, but you'll see it for what it is—you won't shun or resist it.

You'll acknowledge the pain, name it, surrender to it, and allow it to wash over and through you. You'll be able to say "I feel pain," and you will know it in these ways:

+ You will hurt,

+ You will grieve,

+ You might become physically ill,

+ You might become physically affected in unexplainable ways,

+ Your physical body may contract, shut down,

+ You will feel as if you cannot bear it,

+ You will not be able to stop crying,

+ You will feel your spiritual heart cracking open.

At some point in the midst of your suffering and tribulation, you will cry out to the only thing left: Divine/One/All/God/Universe. You will call out in your pain, and in that calling you will ask for relief.

And here, at this juncture, even if you have been numb, stuck, and blocked for years, absolutely certain nothing or no one can help; even if you are sure your pain is too much to bear, too big to be lifted—you will enter the first passage.

THE PASSAGE TO HEALING

In asking, you enter in to Divine space. You allow your heart, ravaged as it is, to be cracked open to Divine light. The Divine takes over when you are spent, done, and have surrendered. At this point, you may only have the energy to open your heart to the smallest sliver of light, the infinitesimally tiniest opening. You may not even have energy for this.

Yet it is enough.

The Divine requires almost nothing of you to begin this first passage, except the asking. What initially happens for most people, is absolute sorrow, grief, and sadness—an enormous release of these emotions. Releasing is always a physical reaction, and may include…

- Crying until you can't cry any more,
- Shuddering, shaking, and convulsing
- Energy surges and feelings of disassociation,
- Stopping of time and a sense of unreality.

And then … even as you are in the midst of the most intense feelings of release, you notice something has changed, such as…

- You may notice a new lightness in the air.
- You may sense energy in the room with you.
- You may discover the presence of God.
- You may see angels, or guides.

- You may see departed loved ones.
- You may see brilliant light.
- You will understand that things have shifted.
- You will notice the absence of pain.
- You will feel the presence of peace.

If you attend to your heart at this moment, you will notice that energetically it has moved from a dark, shrouded mass to a blaze of illumination, a container of light.

This is the Divine healing you.

You may feel shocked by this; utterly blown away.

You may feel a jolt of energy as your pain is converted into something new, something different, something you haven't felt for a long time, if ever.

You may sense the presence of Divine entities—even if you don't believe in them.

You may feel your heart brimming with light—and sadness lifting as the entire reality that surrounds you is changed and lightened.

The healing, when it happens, is instantaneous.

At this time, a few of you will move immediately through all four passages, right into the heart of love. If this happens, hold on! It's an amazing feeling, and consciousness and spiritual awakening will be immediate for you. This ecstatic state may last a few minutes, or longer. A very few of you may remain in this state permanently.

But if you're like most of us, you will soar into this blissful state of heart of love for a few life-changing moments—and then find yourself settling into a new space, a new level or layer of consciousness beyond pain.

This is compassion, the second passage of consciousness that will now permeate your reality.

The 365 Daily Illuminations are designed to help you move through the progression of heart's opening. Use them to guide you as a daily practice, or as inspiration whenever you need comfort, healing, and clarity.

CHAPTER THREE

The Second Passage

HEART OF COMPASSION

 The heart of compassion is felt as a softening, an expansion. It feels as though your entire heart is flooded with love. And yet, the pain is still there; it has not yet transmuted into pure love. This is a time of both the pain ebbing and the compassion flowing.

Kelly was a survivor, but you'd never guess it from her upbeat, generous personality. Underneath that bright optimism was a past filled with enormous pain. She was sexually abused by her father from an early age and her mother, a dysfunctional alcoholic, hadn't done anything to stop it.

Kelly's only way out was to marry young, and on her eighteenth birthday she married Randy, a gentle, hardworking man ten years her senior. Together they raised three children, and by the time I met her they were busy welcoming a new generation of grandkids.

Kelly had done her inner work; she looked at her pain, recognized it, felt it and let it pass through her, and now she was deep into heart of compassion. This great compassion allowed her to recognize pain in others; whenever she sensed pain, she sought to alleviate it.

She'd laugh if you asked her to define her religion, but she prayed continuously to deities from every religion, studied the Bible and other holy scriptures, and took seriously the call to "love thy neighbor as thyself."

By the time I met her, Kelly was well on her way to sainthood.

She was the key volunteer for her family and community, with a mile-long list of responsibilities as she sought new ways to help others. Sun up to sun down, she existed to serve. She'd rise early to check in on a neighbor's dogs and water the lawn, then drive another neighbor to a doctor's appointment, then make the rounds in her community, checking in on the elderly, the poor, the new mothers, seeing who needed help that day. She always had a grandchild or two to baby-sit in the afternoon. When these tasks were through, she'd race through her own household chores, make dinner and talk with her husband, then she'd be off and running again. Some task or volunteer project always kept her busy into the wee hours.

When she first came to see me, it appeared Kelly was brimming with energy. Her vibration was extremely high and she insisted over and over that she was deliriously happy.

"I'm well provided for," she reasoned. "Why shouldn't I help others as much as I can?"

In theory, I agreed … a life of selflessness is often a life of the highest joy. Those who serve others are often the happiest on this planet, but as we sat together, I sensed something different than joy and bliss hovering around Kelly's heart.

At first I couldn't put my finger on it. It was clear that Kelly had moved through heart of pain—she was absolutely clear of her pain of the past. Clearly she was smack dab in the middle of the second passage: heart of compassion. She even said as much herself.

"I feel so much for everyone; I want them to be comforted," she confided. "I know what it is to feel bad, be victimized, and not have help. My childhood is behind me now. I've been blessed beyond measure in my life—and I want to help others who are suffering."

Kelly was a saint in the making when it came to putting others' needs first. This selflessness was true and authentic—her desire to serve was pure.

And yet…

I felt a shadow on her heart. What was this, that I saw or sensed?

It took a while, but finally it hit me: Kelly was in heart of compassion for others, but by subjugating her own needs to those of everyone else, Kelly forgot to hold compassion for one of the most important people in her life: Herself.

A TWO-FOLD OPENING

Jesus said "love thy neighbor as yourself," but the reverse is also true.

In heart of compassion, we open our hearts to two understandings at once:

+ I love everyone, *and*
+ I love myself

Thus, this second passage is two-fold: it includes compassion for others *and* compassion for self. As we move beyond the reach of pain and into the higher levels of consciousness, compassion must exist for all living and sentient beings.

This includes you!

In Kelly's case, with her enormous spirit it was easy for her to feel compassion for the whole world. Now her challenge was to include herself in this great wave of feeling.

First, I asked her to close her eyes, breathe deeply until she was relaxed, and then imagine she was holding the entire world within her heart.

"That's easy," she murmured, "I do this every day."

Next, while she was holding the energy of compassion for the whole world in her heart, I asked Kelly if she could permit herself to be part of this world.

To add herself in.

She paused and her throat made a rough, catching sound. I saw she was crying. These were not the deep, wracking sobs of pain. These were instead the clear, healing tears common to the state of compassion; they ran down her cheeks in an unfettered stream.

Kelly didn't laugh in embarrassment or try to wipe the tears away; she let them flow as we sat for a while in silence.

When we move from pain and enter compassion—compassion being the root of love—we experience free-flowing emotion, including tears. This is what was happening to Kelly.

When Kelly allowed herself to acknowledge how much she deserved and required the same compassion she gave everyone else— that all the deep love she held for the world, she must also hold for herself—at this point of understanding she moved into a state of higher consciousness.

Compassion is the root of love. Compassion is the passage of the heart in which love begins—the point of expansion in which we are released from pain, anger, rage, or hurt, and move into a new dimension. Again, compassion presents as...

- I love everyone, and
- I love myself.

Both aspects must always be present for true compassion to exist.

 In the second passage of the heart, compassion is extended to others and to all living things, but it is also extended to you. You, holding compassion for yourself.

COMPASSION FOR OTHERS

You can easily tell if you are in heart of compassion by how you feel. Common feelings might be…

+ You feel the pain of the world.
+ The world seems heartbreaking to you.
+ You recognize the pain in each person you meet.
+ You are shocked by the pain in the world.
+ You are shocked by the beauty in the world.
+ You sense another's suffering, even if it is hidden.
+ You understand suffering is felt by every a human being.
+ You long to alleviate another's suffering.
+ You want to help, do good, and lend a hand.
+ You feel everything.

When you feel heart of compassion for others, you might do things like volunteer, perform charity work, and help organizations that provide humanitarian aid. Or, you might help on a smaller scale: We assist an older person. We help a child. We care for each other. We work in healing professions of all kinds. We care for strangers who cross our paths.

These are wonderful outpourings of the compassionate heart— to feel the pain of another as your own, followed by the desire to alleviate this pain.

As my client Kelly well knew, service to others brings great joy. Many volunteers say that even though they give lavishly of their time, talent, and treasure to others, they are the ones who receive the real gifts.

When you surrender to compassionate action, that shift changes your life: You get out of the way of yourself, you recognize your own pain as part of the world's pain and release your ego to move deeper into understanding what it means to be human. When you have compassion for others, you might experience the following:

- A sense of duty to a higher calling.
- A sense of vocation.
- The call to serve.
- A willingness to serve in all ways, including lowly or mundane tasks.
- The absence of ego; the ego disappears in the act of service.
- The service becomes the path, the way.
- There is attention to attitude, habit, and actions at a higher level.
- Ego goals such as career, fame, and money will shift or morph.
- You find a new meaning in life.
- The desire to serve others trumps the need for ego success.

Heart of compassion for others is one piece of the puzzle. The next piece, heart of compassion for the self, completes the equation.

COMPASSION FOR THE SELF

Heart of compassion represents a real opening in consciousness; a true advancement into becoming a whole, integrated person. However, while it's easy to hold compassion for others, sometimes we have trouble holding compassion for ourselves.

This is a sticky bit and something not everyone is willing to admit. Many religions and organizations preach only the first part of compassion: that we turn off our egos completely and selflessly focus on the welfare of others. This can become problematic if we take up a false ego of service. We turn into martyrs, servants, and saints. In other words, we care for others more than for ourselves.

But this is not true compassion.

In Kelly's situation, such was the case. Her particular compassion, generous as it seemed, was one sided. She tossed away her own ego to become servant for family, neighbors, anyone who needed help.

Kelly had lived this way for many years. By alleviating other people's pain, she was able to continually affirm that she'd escaped her own painful childhood. "If I am helping others, I do not have to help myself," seemed to be her mantra.

When she came to me, the Universe was asking her to take a different look at what all this selflessness meant. In other words, what compassion did she feel for herself? Not for others—but herself? How was she living her own path, outside the needs of others?

"It feels selfish," she said, as we discussed the idea of living a life outside the helper model. "I feels like it's my ego, and I've been trying to let go of my ego."

I agreed—and yet I also persevered. Each person's life must be lived with full integration—we cannot escape our life's call by taking care of everyone in our path.

With hesitation, Kelly agreed to consider the idea of allowing her compassionate heart to include herself, as well as others—and the Divine took it from there.

From that agreement on, interesting things began happening. Over the next few days she experienced an amazing range of Divine synchronicities, signs, and symbols in the waking and dream state alike.

- She understood herself as connected to family, yet for the first time she also saw herself as a separate being, with her own soul path.
- She understood that in serving only others, she had neglected to serve herself.
- She understood this neglect was actually a way of hiding from her true needs.
- She discovered she truly did have particular life passions, hidden so well and for so long, she couldn't believe they were still there, waiting to emerge.
- She discovered she'd made herself so indispensable to her family that they missed opportunities to learn and grow.

Kelly was shocked by many of these realizations. "But I thought helping others was a good thing," she cried out in our sessions.

Yet she'd learned what she needed to know: that compassion to others is a wonderful thing. But to truly hold compassion in its most complete manifestation, the same courtesy must be extended to oneself. She promised to think more about it, meditate about it, and allow the Divine to come into her heart (something Kelly was already good at doing).

And sure enough, the Divine created change lickety split.

When we next met, Kelly had turned the corner and was living in full heart of compassion: not just a woman who served everyone else, but a woman who also held the deepest compassion for herself.

"I looked at everything, and I decided my real passion was still serving others," she told me. "Except ... I always wanted to do photography. I've wanted to since I was a little girl, but we never had the money for equipment. Later, I was busy being a mom, and then a grandma and volunteer."

The Divine helped reveal this next step.

"It was the strangest thing. I kept seeing cameras after our sessions. I kept hearing "cameras" like a little message in my mind. I kept feeling like a little viewfinder was clicking off in my head." She laughed joyfully. "After a few days of this, I finally clued in— it's the one thing I want to do for myself."

Kelly, to her family's great surprise, became a capable photographer. She still did volunteer work, but she brought a camera with her.

"I see people more clearly through the camera lens," she explained. "I can show their true selves in a way that pleases me, and others."

In allowing herself to have compassion for herself, Kelly was able to find her unique path for soul growth. The life's work of photography was the missing piece for Kelly—something she'd always wanted to explore, but had pushed down in her desire to serve others.

By allowing herself to feel compassion for her self, as well as for others, Kelly was able to truly grow.

WHAT COMPASSION FEELS LIKE

The opening into heart of compassion has a staggering effect—the emotions can be overwhelming. If you're walking around in heart of compassion, be forewarned: you're going to see everyone as if they're naked, fully vulnerable and tender. You'll see them and recognize their suffering; you'll view it with your heart. And, you'll also feel this for yourself.

Jesus said, "Love your neighbor as yourself." In heart of compassion, the reverse is also true: love yourself as your neighbor. Both aspects are required.

In heart of compassion, you recognize yourself as no better—and no worse—than anyone else. Even more important, you begin defining yourself as a human being who experiences suffering, joy, and soul growth in this lifetime—just like everyone else.

Thus, in compassion for others and for self, you might feel...

- A deep sense of the fragility of life,
- A keen understanding of your own mortality,
- A sense of the preciousness of days,
- The realization that you are a product of your sex, race, age, culture, history, and location. Each of these things has affected your life situation,
- Understanding that the past is complete,
- Understanding that all your past mistakes and failings are also complete,
- Understanding you are not perfect,
- Understanding you are not here to be "good" or "pure;" you're holy as you are,
- Loving yourself, in spite of all your faults and flaws,
- Releasing the need to be perfect,
- Having a deep heart opening when you look at your life story as part of the human tale,
- Understanding your struggles as part of the human experience,

- ◆ Having a deep love for yourself as a Divine being having a human experience,
- ◆ Taking time for self-care,
- ◆ Allowing yourself to pursue your passions,
- ◆ Allowing yourself to walk your soul path, whatever this is,
- ◆ Allowing yourself to be you, regardless of what the world tells you,
- ◆ Loving yourself without limitations.

Basically, you stop fighting; you stop trying to be perfect and have everything be perfect. Instead, you look around you in wonder at *what is.*

You simply let go.

When you exist in full heart of compassion—both for others, and for yourself—you start to feel...

- ◆ Relieved,
- ◆ Calm,
- ◆ That everything is going to be okay—or not okay—and you can deal with either,
- ◆ Emotions such as sentimentality, fondness, appreciation, and gratitude,
- ◆ Knowing that every moment is whole and perfect,
- ◆ Trusting in what is to come.

Compassion is a heart resonance with the extraordinary experience of human life: the good and the "bad," all fully integrated.

Each passage of the heart is a gravitational pull toward consciousness. Even when we seem the most stuck, we are continually moving toward love. This is our nature; it is why we are here.

Progression is permanent. Even if we drop back to the first passage of pain now and again, even if we visit anger, rage, and hurt from time to time—once we've gone through the heart of pain and into compassion and the stages beyond, we won't, can't, and don't exist there permanently, ever again.

Once you've tasted higher consciousness, the door swings only one way: toward greater consciousness still.

As you move through the 365 Daily Illuminations in this book, you'll look at compassion, both for others and for yourself. After you've moved through pain, you'll exist in compassion until you are ready for the next passage or opening. Use the illuminations to guide you as a daily practice, or when you need reassurance you are on the right path.

CHAPTER FOUR

The Third Passage

HEART OF CONNECTION

 When you begin to open into heart of connection, you move beyond compassion for your brother, mother, lover, other, and realize we are all the same. You realize that your particular energy is not only of the same essence, it is the same.

Tim's memorial service was the rowdiest I'd ever attended.

The event started with a parade of Harley Davidsons rumbling into the parking lot; about 30 large bikes shining in the sun, leather-clad bikers everywhere, with a deafening thunder. Inside the hall—a spacious building rented to hold hundreds of folks who streamed inside—there was even more noise, chaos, and life.

It seemed representatives from every group on the planet came to pay their respects to Tim. I saw a contingent of police in dress uniform; a band of reggae musicians, middle-of-the-road neighbors who'd known him when he lived in one place or another. I saw classmates he'd known decades before. Friends he'd just made in the last few months. All these people were part of Tim's extended family.

One after another, as the service commenced with a full program of readings, slideshows, singing, crying, and laughing, people stepped up to the microphone and said what they wanted to express about Tim. Everyone was welcome and the stories, though different, were also the same:

"He loved life."

"He was friendly to everyone."

"He always had a hug for me."

"He welcomed me when no one else did."

"He was kind to me."

"He was always there to help."

"He showed up."

"He lived big."

"He loved everything."

Funny—in the years I'd known him, Tim was anything but a saint. Yet in these last remembrances, he was remembered for his kindnesses. He'd recognized each person. He'd shown up. He lived big.

Tim didn't love his job, but he did it. He'd been married three times and was deeply happy with his third wife. He smoked, ate junk food, caroused, and had all kinds of bad habits. He not only wasn't a saint—he never pretended to be one.

If Tim is watching (and he probably is,) he'd laugh at the idea, and then remind me that sainthood was never a job he applied for. In fact, Tim reveled in his human self—the good and the bad and the all of it. On Halloween, and even on days that had nothing to do with costumes, he'd frequently sport devil's horns—little plastic knobs that stuck out of his long, luxuriant hair, causing people to take a second glance. He found the whole thing hilarious

Tim never soared to great heights in a career, made lots of money, or did anything that might be considered ambitious or successful on paper. What he did do was live an ordinary life on a large scale. He was out to have fun, and he did. In fact, his whole life was about embracing joy until, one day in his 50s, after a long motorcycle trip, he climbed off his bike and fell to the pavement, unconscious.

That was the beginning of his end.

He had about a year before the doctor's verdict came in: cancer. Advanced. They tried a few things, but in the end it was too late.

At first, Tim was scared, then angry, then sad—and then an even bigger shift happened, a kind of speeding up of his emotional integration, as he blasted through heart of pain, heart of compassion, heart of connection, and into heart of love, all in record time.

Even though Tim blasted into heart of love and experienced this level of consciousness and the Divine transformation it brings, he didn't stay there permanently. Almost none of us can exist in that level of consciousness for long.

Instead, Tim settled into heart of connection where he stayed the remainder of his journey. He took his adult son on a long promised fishing trip to the sparkling waters of Puget Sound. The trip was exhausting, and yet the photos show him brimming with happiness.

In his final months, he and his wife opened their home to visitors and people flocked to see him in droves. Gaunt and tired to the bone, he saw people every day, turning no one away.

And then toward the end, time transcended for Tim, as often happens to those who inhabit heart of connection. The physical pain didn't go away. But his emotional pain shifted. Heart of connection is about Oneness, which means:

- You move through pain.
- You move beyond compassion.
- You move into the deep understanding of yourself and everyone around you, as one of One.

Tim got Oneness. He spread it like a virus. He lived an ordinary life: work, family, and friends, in a big way. He lived, experienced, and taught through his actions that we are all One. No exclusions. No exceptions. All One. He lived in heart of connection before he knew he was sick—and he spread that legacy like wildfire when he knew his time was short.

Again, you wouldn't call him a saint in his lifetime, but in his soul, he got it, lived it, and became it.

Heart of connection.

One of One.

If you meet a person like this in your lifetime, a person who inhabits heart of connection not just some of the time, but as their way of life … pay attention. The consciousness of this person, his or her great awareness, is a gift to the human race.

HEART OF CONNECTION

We all have some level of consciousness from the moment we are born. To be alive is to be sentient. Animals and living things are sentient, of course. Even other energetic forms we might not consider alive, such as rocks, trees, mountains, the air, and the oceans are sentient in their own way.

Yet as humans, we are blessed with different levels of being conscious.

- In heart of pain (the first passage), you are conscious of your self, your own personal experience.
- In heart of compassion (the second passage), you are conscious of your own humanity, being the same as everyone else.
- In heart of connection (the third passage), you become conscious of yourself as a one of One.

The shift is subtle, and each stage is different:

In pain, you are suffering.

In compassion, you have the idea that you're *the same* as others, having *similar* experiences of suffering, joy, and beauty.

In connection, you move from being *similar* to another, to *becoming* another.

There is no separation; no dividing line.

You exist as a Divine soul, are part of the collective Divine soul.

You're you—but you're also the whole Universe, as God.

You're part of all there is; essence, source, Divine/God/One/All.

And you *are* all there is: essence, source, Divine/God/One/All.

Both at the same time.

It's hard to wrap your mind around this … until suddenly, you can.

 Once you reach heart of connection, everything not in alignment with Oneness falls away; it doesn't matter to you anymore. This shedding of the old can be painful, but it is the only direction you can go.

THE ONENESS PRINCIPLE

In understanding Oneness, most people go through a process something like this: the idea of Oneness doesn't make sense, it seems ridiculous, it all seems a bunch of mumbo jumbo and has no meaning to you personally; it's just pie in the sky rhetoric…

…until one day, you have an experience that changes you,

…and it all becomes crystal clear.

At this shift of understanding, you enter the passage of heart of connection.

In the understanding of Oneness, we understand that we all—not just humans, but everything—are made of particulate energy. Who can say what this particulate energy is? It's beyond the ability of the human mind to comprehend. We can't see it, quantify it, or explain it—yet nonetheless, this particulate energy swirls around continually and constantly in the Divine hum.

This is the God Stuff, the Universe, Source, the *I am That*. All the names you've ever heard for the ineffable essence of One. When we lock into this hum in prayer or meditation, or as we experience the miracle of our daily lives, we understand that everything is energy; nothing is not.

That bowl you're eating cereal from right now is just a loosely gathered collection of energy particulate, with its own particular vibration.

The body you live in? Same thing. It's a bag of chemicals, water, and a soul.

The body is not infinite, but is always changing. Your body will eventually disintegrate. That's how it works.

But the soul is always there. Always One.

When you stand next to someone, your energetic or auric field and theirs will at first touch, and then merge ... the particulate energy extending so it's impossible to tell which is your energy and which is theirs.

Try this sometime at a crowded event or when you have to stand in line with a group of other people. Close your eyes and sense this auric merge between yourself and others.

You'll notice immediately how tenuous, fictional, and imaginary this dream of separate self becomes, when you get down to the level of particulate energy. Because of course, there is no "yours" or "theirs." We're all one big cosmic soup.

Again, this is an abstract concept that means nothing and doesn't make sense until you feel it for yourself. You can experience Oneness intellectually, but until you experience Oneness in your body, as a human, in the only way humans can—in your very human heart, with all its longing, aching, and emotions—you can't really know Oneness.

And often, what's required to bring most of us into this third heart opening, this third passage into Oneness—is nothing short of a miracle.

WHAT HEART OF CONNECTION FEELS LIKE

What do you feel when you are in heart of connection? How do you know you're there? Can you make it happen? Is this the same as a spiritual awakening? These are all common questions for people who are beginning to understand Oneness—not intellectually, but in the heart.

I say "in the heart," because it's easy to nod your head vigorously as various teachers talk about Oneness … and it's quite another thing to move through the passage from pain, into compassion, into connection, where Oneness isn't an abstract idea, but is something you understand so clearly it never leaves you.

In the heart.

Thus, people who experience Oneness usually, if not always, have had deep, intense experiences to get there. These might include…

- Near death experience,
- Being very ill,
- Being in an accident,
- The death of a loved one,
- A personal tragedy,
- A financial loss,
- Getting divorced,
- Breakup of a relationship,
- Losing all material possessions,
- Public shame and humiliation,
- Bottoming out from addiction.

These life events are no fun, but they're often what allow us to break through to a new level of consciousness. When you come close to death—minutes or even seconds away—most of us will have a mystic experience, or a great sensation of God as real. You feel a moment, or moments, of connection and love for every single thing in your life: people, environment, experiences, emotions—all of it.

You recognize everything in one mind-blowing moment, without the blinders or veils we usually wear as we walk around in our daily lives.

You see everything as miraculous. You see everything as God.

And this moment in which you might die, but somehow don't, is often the sparking point for a new life, an awakened life. It's as though you've been gifted with the great secret of the Universe, which is Divine/God/One/All. Once you experience Oneness in this way—emotionally, in the heart— there's no going back.

A COSMIC WAKEUP CALL

In ancient art, angels are often pictured as trumpeting angels, Divine messengers, and heralds of good news. This is what getting a cosmic wakeup call into consciousness feels like—a noisy and insistent angel blasting a trumpet close to your head.

That's the noise part, of this "wake up" call.

There's also the holy part, the sacred part, with the Divine lifting you up in powerful and caring arms, into the place where you rightfully should be. By rightfully, I don't mean because you "should" be conscious because it's the "right" thing to do. We don't need to be spiritual over achievers here. Spiritually opening into heart of connection is not the right thing or the wrong thing to do. It simply what's available to you, if you choose to walk that path.

The miracle of a consciousness shift is profound. Often, it takes the form of…

- ⬥ A life-changing event,
- ⬥ Miraculous events,
- ⬥ Spontaneous healing,
- ⬥ Mystic experiences,
- ⬥ Spiritual awakening,
- ⬥ Bliss, nirvana,
- ⬥ Altered states,
- ⬥ Psychic awakening.

Wow! Sounds pretty nifty, doesn't it? Isn't this what we all strive for—to have mind-blowing experiences? Except—as I've heard time and time again from my clients who've had a spiritual awakening, or who are in the midst of one—as Divine as it is, this experience is no walk in the park.

When we come from a place of such enormous heart expansion and then return to the regular rigomarole of how things are in our daily lives, our routine jobs, with our regular partners ... well, we've changed.

But they may not have.

We've expanded out of our old lives. We busted out of the tin box that once contained our heart. This can be confusing for friends, family members, and even ourselves. I mean, one day you're going about your regular life, not particularly conscious or even quite sure how to get to consciousness, and why would you want to anyway ... and then boom ... you're having a near death experience, you see God, and then...

You have to come back.

To your not very interesting job ... your not very conscious partner ... and the friends and colleagues who don't get what you suddenly can't stop talking about.

Even though it seems no one around you gets it, you know that deep within you at the unshakeable core, you are changed forever—not just for this lifetime, but for all future lifetimes as well.

INTEGRATION: THE STICKING POINT

Integrating this new consciousness can be a challenge as the heart opens continually into more opening. Thus, when you open into heart of connection, your life will change. Like it or not; this is simply what happens, when you experience Oneness.

After spiritual awakening, it's common for people to do things such as...

- End relationships,
- Get divorced,
- Let go of responsibilities,
- Let go of old interests,
- Let go of possessions,
- Lose interest in success and ambition,
- Let go of community,
- Move,
- Quit jobs,
- Divest themselves of everything extra or unneeded,
- Take up a spiritual practice,
- Change habits,
- Change appearance,
- Change friends,
- Wander around in a semi-blissful state,
- Wander around in a full blissful state.

Once you have tasted Oneness, the challenge is integration. Once awakened, you must learn to live with your changed self.

Shouldn't it be easy? Shouldn't Oneness allow you to become even *better* at work, in relationships, and with your family?

Yes ... except there's a huge learning curve when we experience heart of connection. Oneness is so big, so monumental, such an absolute miracle, that we have trouble coming back to earth.

At this point, the best way to become integrated is to practice Oneness in the moment of now. Many of the great teachers of our time, including Ram Dass and Eckart Tolle have talked about the idea of Nownesss and being here Now. When it comes to integrating the earth with the Divine and integrating your experience of Oneness with your life, Nowness is the secret.

Nowness lets you understand fully and know yourself in heart of connection. Yet, instead of blasting off into the etheric realms, never to be seen again, Nowness allows you to come down firmly, feet on terra firm, and literally, be here Now.

In heart of connection, there's a tendency to want to retain the awe, wonder, and magic of experiencing Oneness—which is great. But since the goal of soul growth is to be fully Divine *and* fully human at the same time, you must come down from the ethers and remain earth based.

What does integration feel like? For many people, the experience may include…

- A new life path,
- A new life purpose,
- A new life partner,
- Making amends,
- Healing relationships,
- Spending time alone,
- Spending time in nature,
- Spending time in mediation and prayer,
- Living without fear,
- Loving everyone,
- Detaching from the need to control,
- Detaching from outcome,
- Seeking enjoyment at all levels,
- Having fun,
- Laughing,
- Living in gratitude,
- Living in awe.

In other words, you not only understand connection and living as one in One, but you live it. You let go of anything that does not support the new, expanded you. Your old fearful, controlling, angry, suffering self begins to fade away. You begin living the way a person conscious of him or herself as One would live.

Maybe not all the time.

Maybe not every second of every day.

Certainly, you make mistakes, you slip up, you aren't perfect.

Yet you're able to progressively move toward life as a Divine being, fully conscious as one of One—while at the same time, inhabiting your full human earth self.

And when you move into this place—when you've had the miracle, you've understood the mystery, and now you're trying to live it as a human being, day in, day out—well, then you begin to experience even more.

ONENESS MEANS EVERYTHING

In Oneness, everything is energy particulate, Source/God/All. This includes…

+ People, animals, plants, and all sentient beings,
+ All aspects of nature—mountains, oceans, and air,
+ All non-living things,
+ All aspects of planets, stars, and space,
+ The tiniest minutia of matter.

In other words, we are one with all the tangible things we can see and think about and hold in our minds. But this Oneness principle also extends further to…

+ All relationships,
+ All concepts and ideas,
+ All subsets, groups, and collectives,
+ All dimensions of space, known and unknown,
+ All dimensions of time, known and unknown,
+ All dimensions of consciousness, known and unknown,
+ All other dimensions, known and unknown,

It goes without saying that once you reach heart of connection, psychic abilities are a given. As we experience ourselves and everything around us as One, all aspects of cosmic consciousness become available to us. When we become One we lock into all the secrets and mysteries and hum of the Universe, because *we are also that.*

Entering the third passage—heart of connection—changes you in bigger and more radical ways than heart of pain or heart of compassion. This passage brings about significant shifts, not only in your understanding, but in the day-to-day experiences of your life.

As you move through the 365 Daily Illuminations in this book, you'll explore heart of connection, the idea of becoming one of One. Over time, you'll learn how to exist as One, without separation of any kind. When you work with the illuminations as a daily practice, these ideas will become more clear to you, and you will gain understanding at a new level.

CHAPTER FIVE

The Fourth Passage

HEART OF LOVE

 When heart of connection shifts to heart of love, this is the easiest step because it's a natural expansion. With this shift in vibration, consciousness also deepens. Hold space in heart of love long enough and you become transcendent.

Many years ago I converted to Catholicism as an adult.

Back then, I knew nothing of how my life would unfold. I didn't know I'd have a near death experience, or an unexpected shift in consciousness that would change me forever. At the time, I simply thought joining a religion would help me grow closer to God.

Thus, I went to the first initiate meeting with an expectation that I would grow…

…but I didn't expect the miracle I found there.

All the folks in the group were adult converts like me, but one man stood out. Jack was his name—father of three, with a wife who was a devout Catholic. Jack wasn't converting for himself, he informed the group that day—he didn't feel particularly religious, and he was fine with his current belief system. He was there because it would mean so much to his wife. The other initiates nodded in recognition when he said this. Each of us had our own reasons for joining.

When we met again a month later, I was shocked to see the changes in Jack. His head was completely shaved, with a jagged red scar rounding the top of his head. He'd lost weight too—a lot of it. His clothes sagged on him, several sizes too large, and I wondered why he hadn't made an effort to buy something that fit better.

And there was another difference that I couldn't put my finger on. I could sense it, and I could feel it, but I couldn't name it, because I'd never seen it before.

Jack sat in the semicircle of chairs, glowing as if he'd become radioactive.

"Brain tumor," he explained, smiling broadly at us, as we all tried to come to terms with our shock. "They operated, but it's too late. This is it for me."

His skin was luminous. The air around him was luminous.

We sat rapt in his presence as he continued. "I've had a beautiful life and I'm so grateful to be here with all of you today." And then he beamed at us and the light cascaded out of him.

At that point, whatever we were supposed to accomplish as a group that month got tossed out the window. We settled into our chairs, and were simply *there with Jack.* He glowed, and we basked in his glow. We cried a little. We laughed a lot. He emanated pure love.

Jack was no longer concerned with the details of daily life, he told us; he'd let all that go. And this man who would soon transition out of his earth body, who would soon die, never to see his wife or children or friends or acquaintances again … simply sat there in our midst, an illuminated being emanating light, existing in the pure bliss and love of that exact moment.

It was a great privilege to witness this.

It was an extreme honor to be in his presence.

He radiated like a saint, and in that short few weeks he had transcended in a way most of us will not transcend in our lifetimes.

One minute he was a normal human, with all the usual cares and concerns. The next, he had transmuted into pure bliss, into pure love.

He made a complete passage through all four stages of the heart: pain, compassion, and connection into pure love, in the span of a few days.

A miracle, indeed.

Jack didn't make it to our group initiation ceremony; he died a few days before. The timing didn't seem important. He'd touched us all so deeply with the light that hung around him; not an imaginary light, but a real light that radiated from him. He touched us by the way he held joy, even when he knew his life was ending. Even his wife and children, who were overcome with sorrow because he was leaving, saw this shift, this birthing of a holy being of pure love.

In heart of love, Jack experienced...

- The falling away of everything less than his Divine self,
- His heart opening into everything, a blaze of holy light,
- Absolute communion with Divine as real,
- His ego self-dissolving, so that what remained was a gift to all of us, a shining light of radiance,
- Transmutation of all emotions, even the most painful ones, into pure love,
- The ability to be fully present in Now as it existed in that moment,
- Physical luminosity from his inner essence.

Jack had found the way.

In fact, Jack hadn't just found Source, he had become Source itself. He became Divine essence in a way we do not often see. Indeed, this is something I have witnessed only a few times since;

this blaze of light from the heart, this transcendence of human into Divine while still on this earth.

BEING THERE

We don't have to be near death to experience this kind of spiritual transmutation, although tragedies and illness often open this up in us. It's simply what happens when we move into heart of love, not just for a few moments, but as the way we experience our lives.

If you know how to exist in heart of love—if you've made it through pain, compassion, and connection and landed in heart of love—and if you're able to stay in this state of bliss, nirvana, and enlightenment not just for a minute or an hour, but for all time … please stop reading now and give this book to a friend! You don't need it.

In fact, what I'd really like you to do is call me and be my teacher.

Because while many folks can get into heart of love for a short time, the people who reach heart of love and stay there *all the time* are few and far between on this planet.

Again, most of us know how to find heart of love during brief moments of euphoria, in the miracle moments of our lives. But only the tiniest handful of truly enlightened ones know how to get there and then bask in it—be there and live in it—in every moment of Now.

Not just when it's convenient.

Not just when it feels nice.

Not just when things are going well.

Not just during a workshop, retreat, meditation, yoga class, kirtan, or festival.

Not under the influence.

But all the time.

The challenge of this, the fourth passage, is to achieve this state once, several, or even many times, and then remain in *as a way of being.*

When you exist in heart of love, flow is the only way you can live. When you exist in flow, you exist in effortless enjoyment, effortless integration, and effortless rapture of all that is. You are like a Sufi swirling in bliss, a yogi meditating, a saint in trance—and you exist like this all the time, even as you go about your regular day.

WHAT HEART OF LOVE FEELS LIKE

Even though few of us exist in heart of love all the time, I've been blessed to know many people who exist in heart of love much of the time. These are the folks you absolutely adore meeting: they're fully present with you. They make you feel great whenever you're around them. They make you feel uplifted, encouraged, happy, loved.

Signs of a person who exists in state of love include…

- Absence of ego,
- A deep sense of humility,
- Laughter,
- Joy,
- Openness,
- Sense of humor,
- Grace in doing the simplest, most humble tasks,
- Infinite patience and time for others,
- You feel understood,
- You feel safe with them and have a sense that all is well,
- Deep attention to the task at hand,
- Absolute presence in the moment,
- Deep caring and compassion,
- A quality of seeking to help and heal,
- A different vibration than you're used to,
- Utter lack of concern for everyday things,
- Lack of concern for status and wealth,
- Lack of concern for sexual attraction,

+ Being at ease wherever they are,
+ Always the same in every situation,
+ An advanced emotional range,
+ The ability to feel all emotions at once,
+ Full releasing of the past,
+ No concerns for the future,
+ Connection as a given,
+ Their presence heals,
+ Bliss, nirvana, and euphoria
+ Grace, transcendence, and illumination.

As you can see, people in heart of love don't have time for things like anxiety, panic, crankiness, anger, numbing out, jealousy, or feeling mistreated. They've moved past that pain. They don't have room for feeling everything for the world, or for themselves. They've moved past that compassion.

They don't even have time to wonder about the gifts the state of connection brings: the ideas of Oneness, the consciousness shift that allows intuitive opening, and the transmutation of energy.

They moved past it.

They're beyond all that.

They transcended.

They transmuted.

People in heart of love exist in a higher vibrational state that accepts all pain, compassion, and connection, yet at the same time pays these states absolutely no heed.

In fact, their vibrational state is close to that of a saint, angel, spirit guide, or ascended master or teacher.

Each of you has your own list of people who've transcended their human self and become Divine on earth. When you think about these people, whether you know them in person or by their presence, you'll feel that...

+ They have the most radiant hearts in this world,
+ They may be defined as angels, saints, or holy beings,

- They may be called master or teacher,
- They live in the heart of spiritual mastery,
- They are luminous at all times,
- They exist in enlightenment,
- They have fully integrated all the passages and remain at all times in love.

THE EQUANIMITY OF CONSCIOUSNESS

You'd probably think that opening our hearts would improve our lives. Doesn't it seem logical that as we increase consciousness, we drop old behaviors that make us miserable and manifest new realities that make us happy. Shouldn't we stop attracting "bad" stuff and begin attracting "good" stuff?

Well, yes and no. Higher consciousness doesn't necessarily bring us a "better" life situation, at least in terms of what our mainstream culture considers "better."

Instead, higher consciouness provides us with a new way of perceiving our reality, a new attitude of equanimity. For example...

- When we're in heart of pain, we're stuck. Bad stuff happens and we experience it as more pain.
- When we're in heart of compassion, bad stuff happens but we experience it from the perspective of compassion—for others, and for our self.
- When we're in heart of connection, we understand the interrelatedness of everything and we don't take it personally. As One, we understand we are experiencing collective consciousness, not just our own.
- When we're in heart of love, bad stuff happens, but we don't see it as negative or positive. We just see what *is*. In other words, when we're existing in heart of love, the situation is of no importance.

It's our attitude—our perception—that determines our reality.

THE SITUATION DOESN'T MATTER

"But of course the situation matters," I can hear you saying. Why shouldn't we want great things in our lives? Why shouldn't we want lovely things all the time? Why would we wish a moment's unhappiness for ourselves or anyone else? Surely it doesn't make sense to walk around smiling when things go wrong.

I agree. Across the board, I much prefer nice experiences to rotten ones. And yet, even though it seems easy to swing up into heart of love when we're happy, once we're truly expanded into heart of love, there is no let down, no backward movement, no backsliding, and no downswing, *no matter what happens.*

+ You're in heart of love when things are going great.
+ You're also in heart of love when things aren't going so well.

This seemingly impossible task is attainable to only a few on this planet, and that's why the fourth passage is, for most of us, a hero's quest, our holy grail—the final point on the path of soul growth accessible to us humans at this point in our evolution.

If you're like me, you're still on the path. You're a work in progress, and that progress changes day-by-day, minute-by-minute, during each second of Now.

THE PATH LESS TRAVELED

If you desire to become conscious in heart of love, to live as a being of all love, all the time, you must first go to the beginning, into the pain.

Pain is the starting point.

We have no other place to start from.

If you join an ashram and chant mantras all day with a smile on your face, that isn't starting at the beginning. If you go to divinity school and become a religious scholar, you aren't starting at the beginning. If you travel to India or to wherever the world might take you, that isn't starting at the beginning. You may have spiritual experiences, but you are not starting at the beginning.

If you determine you'll only have a positive outlook and let only positive thoughts and affirmations enter your consciousness, and you tape the phrase "I love myself unconditionally" on your mirror, and you create vision boards, and manifest—that isn't starting at the beginning either.

Unfortunately, "going positive" as I sometimes call it, will not get you into heart of love. That isn't how it works.

Instead, you must burn yourself clear. You must look at all the pain in your heart and deal with that first, before you can open the passages of compassion, connection, and love. No glossing it over, no skipping steps, no jumping ahead … you have to move through the steps in whatever time frame it takes.

ACCELERATED OPENING

Near death experiences, accidents, illness, tragedies, and failings can speed the journey into heart of love. In near death experiences people commonly feel a direct connection with Divine energy. We sometimes hear about a tunnel of white light and the presence of angels or guides, that sort of thing.

During my own experience in 2000, I had a direct connection with the Divine, but I didn't experience a tunnel or white light. I experienced God as golden vibration, a honeyed energy that permeated everything; I knew God in my cells, without doubt or hesitation, in a way I'd never felt before. That's the best I can explain it.

I obviously didn't die with that experience. I was fine. Everything turned out okay in the end. Sometimes I feel silly even talking about it now, this big "near death" that didn't result in death at all.

And yet that experience changed me forever.

While some people who've gone through this have seen the white tunnel, many don't. While some people have a beautiful experience, many recall a frightening one. While some are filled with Divine love on a permanent basis or become instantly psychic, healed, or enlightened, many do not.

I did not.

I did not become infused with love. I did not become healed. Instead, I fell into a deep spiral of posttraumatic stress and fear. And yet ... even though my progress was excruciatingly slow, even though the Universe seemed to banish me directly into the pit of pain ... this is where I began.

In entering pain, which I'd avoided until this time, my opening began. And thus, the most horrible experience of my life forced me to descend into heart of pain in a fast, furious, non-negotiable way ... and in this manner I encountered an accelerated process.

This is my journey; I didn't choose or ask for it. It just happened. Others who've known tragedy, illness, or some great crisis have also felt this kind of acceleration.

You've had your own experience.

If you are a person who was born in heart of love, and there may be a few people like this on the planet—you don't need to be accelerated.

But if, like most of us, you've been avoiding your feelings, distracting yourself, and denying who you are and what you're doing with your life (as I was), it's likely you'll receive a wake-up call—an "Aha!" moment that gets you down to business fast.

When we face death, tragedy, or sudden, inexplicable change; when we look at the idea of finite time ... this brings a cognizance that changes everything.

When we face the knowledge that we will die, when we recognize the container of our life as finite ... we learn to live our lives in a whole new way.

We drop out of ego and self, and see ourselves as we really are—as a soul wearing a body. And with this cognizance everything becomes amazing: a tree, a flower, a cup of coffee, the warm covers on the bed. All our experiences become amazing. And of course, all our dear ones become the most precious things in the world.

This gratitude, this entering into bliss, is where we join the consciousness of nirvana, enlightenment, and love. Our hearts instantaneously expand into this realization.

If we're lucky, we transcend and transmute, so that we stay in heart of love forever.

If we're on a slower path, we're gifted with a glimpse of this miracle of enlightenment, a brief moment of knowing … and then we return to our regular lives, to move forward with new knowledge.

But this glimpse!

This glimpse of everything as God/One/All/Divine, even for only one second, is enough to open and change us—if not to the point of living in heart of love all the time, at least enough to experience a psychic and spiritual awakening; at least enough to let us exist from that moment, knowing we have seen God and understood all energy.

And with that viewpoint, we will never be the same.

ENTERING BLISS

Everything changes after the moment of the great "Aha!" You've seen it, you know it, and you moved from pain, into compassion, into connection, and you even made it into love…

You've had a spiritual awakening.

You've achieved conscious cognizance of love; a recognition in energetic and vibration and emotional form of God/One/All/Divine/Universe, everything all the time, the sacred hum, the web, the alpha and the omega.

You've seen it, you know it, you felt it, and your heart expanded so quickly and grew so large it was beating outside your body, burst right through the confines of your human chest.

You transmuted from human into Divine.

You are in heart of love.

And then what?

What happens after love, which feels like bliss, nirvana, and illumination? What happens after you've walked around with this feeling for a few minutes, a few hours, a few days, even for months on end, with no let-up in this feeling?

Eventually, unless you are a saint or holy one—in which case you get to hang out in love nonstop until the end of time and may at the point of self-realization evaporate into thin air—you'll have to integrate.

If you're like most of us, at some point this love consciousness will subside. You'll go to the place Buddha calls "chop wood, carry water." In a more modern turn of phrase, Jack Kornfield titles it "after the ecstasy, the laundry."

And not just the laundry!

But also the dishes, the dog walking, the grocery shopping, the dental appointments, the mortgage payment, and the hundreds of mundane tasks that may not seem Divine at all.

And yet, here we are.

Back again in the Now.

Sometimes, when we have that great "Aha!" and become infused with the sweet mystery of love, and we feel it and know it ... well, that's when this "back to the laundry" let down happens and we feel something new; something akin to grief.

It's lovesickness for the Divine.

It's a heartbreaking longing for the nectar of Source.

It's the unquenchable desire for something we had the merest glimpse of, but was all we've ever wanted.

It's a journey you want to take again and again—nothing else matters, nothing could be more meaningful.

Hence, we become pilgrims, we become renunciates to all that is not love. We become passionate in our pursuit of heart of love. Such was the longing of the great poet Rumi and all the saints and mystics throughout the ages; of the many today who dance and chant and sing and meditate; of the many who follow no practice, but laugh and enjoy and are the true bhaktis of the world

This is how we become when we enter heart of love.

STAYING IN

One moment in heart of love and your life permanently changes. One taste, and you want that sweetness forever. I know how you can enter, but I cannot teach you how to stay in this state of bliss, nirvana, and Divine infusion.

I can only offer this: the more you enter, the more often you allow yourself to become infused with the Divine, whether you do this by prayer, meditation, nature, service, or by always choosing love, as many times a day as you can. The more you enter into this state, the more it becomes your reality.

Divine infusion changes us. This is the nature of the Divine. When our hearts are opened into love—even one time—we are transformed forever.

This is the life's journey. This is the journey of soul growth; to enter heart of love early and often, and to claim reality as your own reality, for all the moments of your life.

And it isn't just for you. It is for you, as teacher, to spread this expansion, this consciousness, like a contagion so that heart of love is not theoretical, but active, dynamic, and real enough to move into the consciousness of all sentient beings. Be in heart of love, now.

When you forget, when you slide back ... simply breathe, and enter again.

And when you forget the next time ... breathe yet again. Enter in anew.

There's no other secret.

There's no other way.

This is your life's journey of soul growth to grace.

It's all there is.

Turn now to the 365 Daily Illuminations, and begin your journey into consciousness. Use the illuminations to guide you in your heart's opening, each day opening into further expansion and joy. .

PART TWO

365 Daily Illuminations

These illuminations are the sequel to *The 33 Lessons*, the spiritual teachings I received in 2008. As my first experience with Divine receiving, these early teachings emanated from three guides who taught that the purpose of life is soul growth. The teachings were published in my book *Writing the Divine*.

Three years after that first receiving, I once again found myself serving as scribe for the Divine. This time the messages focused on a new concept—an idea that was touched upon in *The 33 Lessons*, but was now expanded and developed in a more specific way. In a nutshell, the teachings stated that not only is soul growth the purpose of life, but that *soul growth happens through the human heart.*

As I sat with eyes closed and laptop open, writing the messages as they arrived to me over a period of several months, the guides stated clearly and persistently that the heart's opening into consciousness was not only a progressive opening, but specifically sequential—a series of four passages that led to enlightenment.

With great joy, I now offer these teachings to you for illumination, comfort, and healing.

HOW TO USE THE ILLUMINATIONS

Designed as a year-long course of study, these daily inspirations will take you through an understanding of the process of soul growth via the four passages of the human heart. Each lesson includes a spiritual teaching followed by a contemplation to be answered in writing, prayer, or meditation.

The result? Heart's opening, personal transformation, and a profound shift in consciousness and vibration.

These daily teachings offer a progressive understanding of the human experience of soul growth. However, that does not mean growth will come each day.

At times the lessons will make sense and feel profound. At other times (especially at the beginning,) the lessons will hold no meaning for you—they will simply not make sense, or may not seem to apply to you. You may even feel they're written in a foreign language.

Stay with it.

As you immerse yourself in the Divine vibration of these teachings, you will notice things beginning to shift. As your heart opens through the four passages and as your consciousness expands, your understanding will increase.

After a few days of this immersion you will notice yourself relaxing more easily and experiencing more joy. In a few months you will notice the circumstances of your life begin to change in a positive manner. By the end of the year you will be astonished and grateful for the miraculous transformations that have taken place.

Be patient. Detach from outcome. Simply do the practice and allow the Divine to work as it always does.

A DAILY PRACTICE

There are 365 teachings; you may begin at any time.

Each day, hold yourself in a quiet space and read the teaching from a state of openness. Allow your consciousness to connect with the Divine and you will remember what you already know.

When you finish reading the daily lesson, write or think about the question that follows. If you like, close your eyes and take a deep breath in through the nose and out through the mouth, until you feel yourself entering a state of deep relaxation. Then, contemplate what you receive. This may include thoughts, memories, emotions, images, sounds, and feelings—allow it all in.

How long should you spend on each teaching? For some, five minutes in the morning will be just enough—a blessed way of beginning and centering your day.

For others who wish to go deeper into the practice, a longer session of contemplation, prayer, and journaling will feel just right.

There is no set recommendation—you will know what is right for you.

Also feel free to use these teachings in a less structured way—as guidance for any situation you find yourself in. Allow the Divine to choose your teaching "at random" as you open to any page and let the teaching speak to your heart.

And now, let us begin.

1

BEING BORN IS A PASSAGE OF FORGETTING; everything you once knew disappears, must be relearned again. This is the soul's purpose: this continual movement toward consciousness, toward remembering. In this lifetime, in every lifetime, this is your soul's destiny.

Do you know what your destiny is? Close your eyes right now, and breathe in through your nose, out through your month. Allow the idea of your soul's purpose to appear to you. Receive the information that arrives.

2

THE FIRST PERSON YOU SAW WAS YOUR mother or father. This was the first relationship. And yet other relationships in your life have been equally destined. Those in your soul circle have come to join you in this lifetime.

What are your key relationships in this lifetime? Write the names of these people. Also, if you can, write the lessons you are learning with them.

3

YOU WILL HAVE MANY KARMIC CROSSINGS in this lifetime. Those who surround you now are familiar to you; you have known them before. If you are jumping levels of consciousness in this lifetime, some may be new.

Consider now who is with you on your journey. Again, what are your karmic lessons with each person on your journey?

4

THE IDEA OF TIME IS PURE MIRAGE. Time exists in the same energy plane as all energy. Thus, it is created of particulate energy, infinitely expanding and contracting.

How does time work for you now? Do you have enough? Too much? What if time did not work in this way at all?

5

TIME IS NOT LINEAR. It is energy, and energy does not work that way. Thus, it is easy for you to jump levels in time: to visit this lifetime in the past, that event in the future. For example, it is simple for you to understand who you still hold karma with in this lifetime. Simply by closing your eyes, you may begin to see a glimpse of the last lifetime you had together.

Understand that linear time is a fallacy. Thus, whatever you would like to experience in this moment is the most important consideration you can have. How would you like to enjoy time? In what way would you like to live?

6

IF YOU ONLY HAD ONE DAY LEFT in this lifetime, how would you spend it? What if you had one year?

Write these thoughts down and let them inform you.

7

OUR SOUL IS INFINITELY COMPLETE; it is our Divine container. We are always soul, one with One. Yet in earth life, in the human experience, the heart is the way in which we grow.

Do you feel your heart is open today, or closed? Close your eyes, breathe, and ask your heart to tell you.

8

WE GROW BY OPENING OUR CLOSED HEART up to ourselves, to one another, and finally, to the deepest, most profound aspect of the Divine. These are the four passages of the heart that lead to soul growth. No other method is possible.

Close your eyes and breathe in through your nose, out through the mouth, until you are gently relaxed. Again, picture your own human heart. How open is it? How closed? How open would you like it to be? How far can you allow it to open today?

9

WE ARE HERE TO TEACH EACH OTHER lessons in soul growth. This can be pleasant or uncomfortable. With those in your soul circle, those with whom you have karmic crossings, you will understand the destined aspect of this relationship, even from the moment of meeting.

What lessons have you already learned in this lifetime? With whom is your karma complete, meaning you have learned that lesson with them already?

10

KARMIC CROSSINGS ARE ALWAYS STRONG. They may be difficult, they may be memorable, and there is always a sense of attraction or repulsion that cannot be resisted. They may be long lasting, or short and immensely strong, depending on how fast you learn the lesson.

What relationships are you working on most today? This week? What relationships do you avoid working on?

11

YOUR BODY IS NOT A RANDOM CONTAINER. It is chosen by the soul before you arrive into this earth life. It is also a place in which you will learn lessons.

What particular aspects of your body do you enjoy? What do you dislike? What aspects bring you joy? What makes you feel sad, ashamed or disturbed?

12

YOU MAY IMAGINE YOUR OWN BODY as a baby, a tiny infant. Do you see how you can hold this baby in your arms, near to your heart? You may also imagine your own body as an aged person, the day before your death. Do you see how you can hold this aged person in your arms, near to your heart?

Your body is a Divine container that will change over your lifetime. Revel in this! Notice it! This is the way of things: the softening of the shell so the soul may emerge.

13

WHERE YOU LIVE IS NOT A RANDOM CHOICE. It is chosen by the soul, as part of your life's path. You will be happiest if you live in a place that matches your vibration most completely. You will be unhappy if you are out of vibrational match.

Do you enjoy the land on which you live? Why or why not? Are you in correct vibration with the earth in the area, region, and home where you live?

14

RECALL THE PLACES YOU HAVE LOVED BEST. Were you with forest, ocean, desert, or mountains? Were you north, south, east, or west? You are always called to the place your particular soul requires as home in this lifetime.

Close your eyes and imagine yourself in this beloved place. Ask this place if you need to return now, or later, or if this is complete for you.

15

SIN IS A CULTURAL MISBELIEF. The concept of being punished for sins isn't required by you. Morality is a cultural construct, not a Universal law.

What sins do you have? Make a list. Ask yourself if these are truly sins, or if they are just part of the human condition.

16

THERE IS ALWAYS LIGHT, AND ALWAYS DARK, and as a human being there is never a time these two do not coexist and commingle. Both aspects create a whole; this is integration.

How would your life change if you allowed yourself to believe both in your Divine imperfection and in your Divine perfection?

17

YOU MAY HAVE REGRETS IN YOUR LIFE. But regrets do not mean failure; regrets show that you have learned. The purpose of life is soul growth—learning, through the heart's opening, is the point.

Do you still need to call this a regret? Are you able to love the person you were then? Are you able to love the person you have become?

18

FORGIVENESS IS A CULTURAL IDEA, and it is not of use. There is only energy, and that energy is either light or dark, hot or cold, gathering or releasing, or in point of change—in he process of moving between two states.

Write down what you think you should be able to forgive by now. Tear up the list. See what happens today.

19

ROMANTIC LOVE IS ONE OF THE GREATEST DELIGHTS of this lifetime. Those who experience the tantra of Divine union with another know God.

With which other souls have you known God in this way? Think on this now.

20

TRUE TANTRA IS POSSIBLE whether the relationship is long or short, sanctioned or unsanctioned, proper or improper. The karmic crossing is what determines tantra; not society.

Think about how your tantra experiences have changed you, opened you, and transformed you. If you have not experienced this, would you like to?

21

THE MARCH OF DAYS WE USE in this lifetime is not a useful way of measuring a life. More happens in the moment of watching a blade of grass blow in the wind, or in noticing the soft warmth of another's body, than in countless months of schedules, work, or progress.

What have you noticed today? Open your eyes! Notice something beautiful, heartbreaking, profound, and extraordinary. This is how life is all the time.

22

THE ANIMALS WE HAVE AS "PETS" are not here to serve us. They have come to assist us. Their soul contracts are the same as ours—to come into family, home, place of being, and move through what they are here to experience.

What pets do you have? Think about them today.

23

IN MANY CASES, OUR PETS HAVE COME to heal us by reminding us to relax, open our hearts, and to love. They understand clearly how fragile we are.

If you have pets, can you sense them communicating with you even now? What do you believe they are here to help you with?

24

WHEN YOU WERE SMALL YOU HAD A DREAM. This dream, this early dream, is often the beginning of remembering the soul path you have agreed to walk; the journey that is this lifetime's destiny.

What did you love when you were seven, ten, or twelve?

25

CONSIDER YOUR AGE. How many years do you believe you will live? If you start now, you still have time to live your dreams.

Do you believe you have enough time left? Consider how much time you truly need.

26

IF YOU HAVE ALREADY STARTED to move into your dreams, recall for a moment the ways the Universe has helped you step onto your path.

We do not move through life alone. Make a list now of all who have helped you create your dreams. Be in gratitude.

27

EVERYTHING THAT HAPPENS IS A DIVINE CONVERGENCE: the meeting of you and another, the place, the sign, the synchronicity, all at the same exact moment when you are awake, aware, paying attention.

A synchronicity is about to happen today. Be awake!

28

THE DIVINE GIVES US STRANDS: links or chains of synchronicities that lead us to our highest possibility. When you see a synchronicity, follow it. Allow it to lead you to the next.

A synchronicity will also happen today. Follow it!

29

MIRACLES AREN'T MAGIC; they are merely conscious creation; they are energy intended. Miracles are manifestations, and you can choose to create them in any and all aspects of your life. The moment you believe this, it begins to happen.

What have you been asking for lately? What have you been getting? What would you really, really like? Ask for it today.

30

IF YOU AREN'T HAPPY WITH YOUR LIFE, why are you living it this way? Do you understand that this lifetime is not meant to be safe, simple, easy, and secure? It's a lavish feast, filled with everything of which you might wish to partake. Taste it!

Today, lose your fear and take a bite. Fill yourself in this lifetime.

31

WHEN WE ARE STUCK, WE ARE REALLY SAYING "No." There is nothing to say no to. There is nothing to resist. All is experience: soul growth through the opening of the heart.

What do you say no to? Why? What would you like to say yes to? Is there any reason you cannot do this?

32

BEING HERE NOW MEANS BECOMING AWAKE and staying awake. It's easy to doze off in the routine of schedules, to-do lists, shoulds, fears, fantasies, and addiction. If you're truly awake, life looks like a whole different animal.

How awake are you today: Ten percent? Forty percent? Ninety percent? What do you need to become fully awake?

33

WHEN YOU'RE AWAKE, YOUR EYES will always be popping out of your head because this life is so insanely glorious. If you don't see this vibrant, wild, amazing glory, you need to wake up.

Close your eyes and imagine a tiny cup. Look and see how full the cup is. Just a little? Half full? To the brim? Overflowing? This is how awake you are today.

34

YOU CAN LOOK AT MONEY AS PIECES OF PAPER, circles of metal, and numbers in a computer. Or, you can view money as energy. When you choose to see money as energy, you will lose the desire to worry about "how much' or how many "pieces" of money you own.

How do you see money? How much do you need to have enough? Are you sure?

35

WHEN YOU LOOK AT MONEY AS ENERGY you understand how easy it is to manifest and create the energy of money. You will do this easily as your heart opens.

Write down your biggest fears around money. Ask yourself, "Do I need to keep these fears." If you are ready to release them, do so now. Simply write "I am ready to release my fears around money."

36

ABUNDANCE MEANS HAVING ENOUGH—so much "enough" that you feel sated, happy, and full. Society tries to present us with a particular view of abundance. But abundance means different things to different people.

Don't be fooled by what society tells you. Determine your own needs.

37

YOUR OWN NEEDS FOR ABUNDANCE are physical/material, emotional, and spiritual. You may be full in some areas, while in others, you may be hungry.

What would make you fully abundant? After you answer this question the first time, ask yourself if this is your highest truth. Then, answer the question again.

38

SUCCESS IS A MYTH. There are only experiences. When you reframe your concept of success as experiences you would like to create, everything changes.

Take a moment and reframe your idea of success. What does it mean to you? What does this look like to you?

39

STOP COMPARING YOURSELF; you are not another soul. You are here to create exactly the experiences you most need in this lifetime. Each soul walks its own path.

Of whom are you envious? Take a moment, and understand this person as a whole person with a unique path. Take a moment and appreciate yourself this way, too.

40

WE HAVE BEEN LED TO BE BELIEVE that more, bigger, faster, stronger is what we should desire. This is a lie. The Divine leads us to what we need. This may be less, smaller, slower, or weaker.

The Divine leads us to what we need. Where have you been led lately? What resonates?

41

YOU ARE MEANT TO ENJOY YOUR CORE SELF. Delight in your core self! To do this, you must divest your need to fit in, to compete, to be "better." Just let it go, like a balloon turned loose to sail on the wind.

Who are you "better" than? Who is "better" than you? How do these beliefs serve you?

42

YOUR OWN PARTICULAR NEED FOR EXPERIENCES is determined by your soul's path: you will be led to the experiences that are your highest possibility. Once you start to trust this, it makes putting one foot in front of each other much easier.

Do you know where you're going? If you have no idea, how does it feel to walk blind? Can you let go and trust?

43

WE DO NOT GET A BIG MAP of our life's journey when we're born. We are meant to wander, explore, and journey in the direction our heart points us.

Where are you now, exactly today? Look back on your life's journey and recall how you got here. Is this enough to trust that you will be moved forward with equal grace?

44

UNDERSTANDING THAT WE ARE SOMETIMES moving forward in flow, sometimes gathering information, and sometimes resting for the next leg, will make your trip much more fun.

What state of movement are you in now: Resting? Gathering? Flow? Do you understand these are a cycle?

45

THIS SOCIETY PROMOTES THE ILLUSION that you have absolute control over your life. It is true, you may consciously create; but only in partnership with the Universe. At no time are you alone in charge.

How much control do you think you can have over your life? Are you sure? What if the Universe has a better plan for you than you have yet imagined?

46

THIS IDEA OF MEASURING A LIFE by earth standards? It's ridiculous. The heart's opening is the only thing that matters in this lifetime. There's nothing more.

Check again: how open does your heart feel today? If you feel scared, stressed, unloved, or disappointed, you are ready to open your heart. Do it now. Feel the expansion and the relief.

47

THE HEART IS CLOSED IN FOUR WAYS: first by the physical body, next by the emotional armor we all carry, and then by the physical heart itself. Finally, at the very center of everything, is your inner heart, the heart within your heart: *Ananda Khanda.* This is what desires to be cracked open to the world. Recall the heart within your heart, your *Ananda Khanda.* Rest with this. Even if your heart is fully locked away now, it can be opened.

Recall the heart within your heart, your Ananda Khanda. *Rest with this. Even if your heart is fully locked away now, it can be opened.*

48

DO YOU THINK OPENING YOUR HEART will hurt? The moment the light comes in may feel overwhelming. But after that, you will feel immense relief.

Just today, imagine your physical body that covers your heart is opened. Imagine your chest cleaving open and light spilling into the next layer.

49

SOME PEOPLE PUT ON HEART'S ARMOR every day, imagining the more they put on, the safer they will be. Of course, this is misbelief. The more you can open your heart, open to the heart within your heart, the more joyous, complete, and transcendent you will be.

Write down your preferred method of heart's armor. If you believe you are completely open, completely transparent, look again.

50

WHY DO WE HAVE TO OPEN OUR HEARTS? Why can't we stay in the comfort zone and not be force to feel everything, all the time? Well, we can. Many people do. This is a point of choice for each human in every lifetime.

Are you at the point of choice now? Hold this thought today and see how the Universe informs you.

51

IF YOU FEEL CRANKY, UNHAPPY, CONFUSED, or in fear, these are sure signs that you are ready to open your heart. If you feel stressed, afraid, or deeply sad, these are also signs.

Are you ready to move beyond fear and sadness in this lifetime? Do you think you could do this now, or do you need to do it later? When is the right time for you?

52

THE HEART OPENS OVER AND OVER AGAIN, until the heart within the heart, the *Ananda Khanda*, is finally able to become illuminated and infused with light. These openings happen in the most ordinary moments of every lifetime.

What have you opened to this week? What have you resisted?

53

WHEN THE INNER HEART OPENS FULLY, this is known as bliss, transcendence, or nirvana. There is no going back from this opening; the inner heart, once opened, always remains open. If this happens to you, your life will be forever changed.

Do you desire to have your inner heart, your Ananda Khanda, *opened? If you do, please ask for this now.*

54

NO ONE WILL COME TO FIX YOU: not your mother, brother, lover, or anyone else. You may only choose to heal yourself while others stand by as witness to your human experience on earth. The sooner you understand this, the sooner you may begin to heal.

Who do you depend on? Who depends on you? Have these relationships grown, or are they stuck?

55

WHEN YOU SEE PEOPLE HEADING down the wrong path, what should you do? Only what you would do for any fellow traveler who is lost: Point out a new direction, provide a flashlight for illumination, share your snack. Each person walks his or her own path of soul growth.

Who have you been trying to "fix" lately? Is it working? If you knew the result would be the same whether you "fixed" or released your need to fix, what would you do?

56

YOU CREATE YOUR REALITY with your consciousness. When you are in fear, in lower vibrations, your consciousness is constrained. When you are in joy and love, in higher vibration, your consciousness creates effortlessly.

Do you belief you create your own reality? What if it were true? How would you change your life if you knew this was true?

57

WE MAY BE GROUNDED IN EARTH BODY, but the heart is what rules us. Our emotions are mutable, changeable, and fickle, not to be trusted. Yet, at the same time, they are deep, profound, and breathtaking. They always change, shift, and move like a leaf in the wind or waves in the ocean.

How do you use your feelings? Can you see that because emotions are always in a state of flux, you must use them differently than you would use a static tool?

58

EMOTIONS ARE LIKE SAILS; they must be adjusted as each breath of wind arrives. Tighten them too far and the boat capsizes. Let them out too fast and the result is the same. Learning to sail with your emotions is one of your lessons.

Think of something that makes you cry. Think of something that makes you ecstatically happy. Now, shift quickly from one emotion to another, six times. Sometime today you will find use for this tool.

59

THERE ARE FOUR PASSAGES OF THE HEART you may experience in this lifetime. They are: pain, compassion, connection, and love. Each opening is progressive, leading you to the next.

Does the passage into pain sound as though it will hurt? It will not. You will feel tremendous relief when you finally release all that pain.

60

IN HEART OF PAIN, THE FIRST PASSAGE, you will become awake to your own pain and to the pain of others; this is the first step of opening, awakening and becoming a conscious being.

Would you rather face this first passage of pain or remain stuck? The choice is yours.

61

IF YOU SEEK CONSCIOUSNESS, there is nowhere to go but through the pain. Pain is not the easiest passage. But with the full experience of the pain you have experienced as a human on this earth, you begin to transform.

Have you felt pain in your life? Of course, the answer is yes. Have you allowed the pain to move through you, or are you still holding it away from your heart?

62

SOME OF YOU HAVE BEEN THROUGH the heart of pain already. Some of you have locked your hearts away for a very long time. There is no right or wrong state. You are where you are. There is only expansion, opening from here.

If you have already moved through the heart of pain, recall this experience. If you feel you are ready to begin, ask to do so.

63

AWAKENING INTO THE AWARENESS OF PAIN is like a numb person becoming conscious. This opening is similar to a sliver of light finding its way through the many wrappings of the heart: first the outer cocoon of the body, then the armor we all put up, then the actual physical heart, and finally into the inner heart: the heart of hearts.

Just for one moment, open your heart through all the layers. Allow yourself to hold the pain, feel it, and then release it. In this very action, you are transformed.

64

WHEN THE HEART OF HEARTS IS ILLUMINATED by Divine light, even if it is the smallest sliver of light, everything begins to change.

Imagine, today, that a sliver of Divine light has found its way into your heart. Close your eyes, breathe deeply, and hold the picture in your mind's eye of the light finding its way into your heart. Allow yourself to feel what you feel.

65

MANY TIMES, PEOPLE TRY TO NUMB themselves from the opening into pain, by drugs, alcohol, food, politics, money, exercise, sex, shopping, or media: all the many, many distractions of life. The diversions serve to distract, but they do not allow the heart to open.

What addictions do you have? What problems have they solved for you?

66

YOU MAY CHOOSE TO DISTRACT because you feel the opening into pain may be too difficult for you to bear. This is not so. The opening into pain, the first truth of what you have suffered, is a Divine relief.

Understand that the progressive opening of your heart will make you feel better. Think about this today.

67

WHAT DO YOU DISTRACT YOURSELF WITH? What do you do obsessively, as habit? These habits may even be useful, good, and healthy. Still, they may also be attachments that distract you from opening, from true awareness.

What good habits are a distraction for you? Write these down.

68

THE PERSON WHO DOES YOGA for hours each day or the person who obsesses over organic food, may well be as distracted as the person who uses drugs, alcohol, junk food and so on. All attachments are ways of distracting from your real purpose, which is to open into the light.

What if you didn't do any "good" things today? What resistance arrives to you with this idea?

69

THE IDEA OF BEING "GOOD" IS USELESS. Human beings are both sacred and profane, Divine and earthly. The integration of these two sides is what's important—to accept your whole self, your whole person.

How attached are you to the idea of being Divine, holy, good, nice, or healthy? Do you think this idea is true?

70

EACH PERSON ON EARTH CONTAINS a shadow side: your anger, pessimism, fear, and anxiety. It is through integrating this shadow with all the ideas you hold "good" that you become truly Divine.

Close your eyes and picture this shadow on the left of you and your Divine self on the right. Slowly, allow these two energy forms to merge into the center of your body.

71

ANIMALS HOLD NO MORALITY, no shadow; they are fully integrated beings. So too, are babies, plants, rocks, the wind, the trees, the mountains, and all of nature. In full integration, you simply are what you are. This is Divine!

Today, look for "good" trees, or "bad" trees. Do you see how this concept does not apply? The same is true for you.

72

THE FIRST PASSAGE OF THE HEART, that of pain, is a shift many people find overwhelming. It is not the passage itself that seems overwhelming, but the thinking about it—the fear of it. That is why so many people fight this passage so desperately, until the Universe takes matters into its own hands and causes this shift to happen.

Have you had a catastrophe lately? Personal chaos? In what ways have these experiences been gifts? What have they taught you about yourself and who you are? If you have moved through the passage of pain already in your life, recall this time for a moment, and then recognize where you are now.

73

WE ALL WILL HAVE FEAR AND JOY, sorrow and love, in waves of repeated cycles throughout our lives. However, the first passage into pain is the first opening into consciousness. It is the first time we begin to awaken.

Consider how you have become more whole as you've become more awake. If you have not yet awakened, if these words mean nothing to you, then close your eyes and ask the Universe/Divine/One/All to assist you with light.

74

WITH THE FULL ALLOWING, the full experience of all the pain in our lives and in our world, we feel everything. We feel all the pain we thought our hearts could hold—and yet, we do not die. We are still here. This is the first opening into awareness.

The first step of the heart of pain is allowing yourself to feel everything fully, without distraction. Try it now by thinking of something moderately painful in your life. Just feel that emotion fully. Recognize that it was not too much.

75

YOUR HUMAN HEART CAN HOLD EVERYTHING. Your Divine soul is both everything and beyond everything. Allowing this first passage to happen, descending down and into pain, is what allows you to understand your full being as human and Divine.

Close your eyes, and think now of the most painful things in your life. Feel this pain fully. When you are done, open your eyes and begin to live your life again.

76

WHEN YOU HAVE MOVED INTO the first passage of pain, you will see pain everywhere. This is a temporary state. You will see pain in all beings who are distracted and numb, and you will see pain in all beings who are in the pain state.

Notice today who is in pain around you. You will be shocked by how many people you see.

77

RECOGNIZING THAT YOU ARE NOT ALONE, that you are not different, that pain is universal before and during the first opening, is useful to you.

Take a walk and head to an area where you are with other people. Become aware of the numbness, the distraction, and the pain in this collective energy. Observe it. Know that you are not alone.

78

MOVING THROUGH THE PAIN STATE sometimes takes months, and even years. But often, it is quick. People who have been ill, in accidents, lost their jobs, or lost relationships often open and transform very quickly.

Are you getting tired of pain? Are you ready to move forward? Ask the Divine to accelerate you, in your progress.

79

YOUR ABILITY TO FEEL PAIN and move into the next stage is based on how willing you are to let go of fear. When you feel pain, most of you will contract and become filled with fear, which is also pain. Instead, you may choose to expand into the pain.

When you're ready, your passage through pain can be nearly instantaneous. Are you ready?

80

IF YOU DON'T WANT TO STAY IN PAIN, you first need to fully experience your own pain. And then, you may expand out of it. You can't go around it: Only through.

Take a few days and review all the pain in your life. Feel it fully. Then, release it. Just let it go. This is possible, and it is not a miracle. That's how energy works.

81

IT IS IMPOSSIBLE TO REJECT PAIN, reject suffering, and only live in light, without first passing through the pain. This is the nature of the human heart: light cannot be attained without the first cracking open of the heart.

Want to skip steps? You can't. Notice your resistance to this.

82

IT IS IMPOSSIBLE TO SKIP STEPS in this process of opening, though you may go through the steps very, very fast. It is possible for this process to be instantaneous.

The Universe is energy; energy has no time. If you are ready to open today, feel the pain—and move forward forever.

83

THE SECOND PASSAGE OF THE HEART is compassion. When you have moved through the heart of pain you'll find yourself in a new place. It is tremendously lighter here! You are now in the second passage of opening. The Universe sends its congratulations.

Things go much faster from here! Close your eyes and allow yourself to feel compassion for the first person who comes into your sphere of reality today. Note how this is different from feeling pain; note how the vibration is different.

84

IN MANY HOLY TEACHINGS, the idea of compassion is misrepresented as the final stage of evolution. This is not so. Compassion is merely a stepping stone to what comes next. You can go higher if you wish. Most of you will.

Feel compassion for every living thing you can sense or see today. Simply expand your heart. Do this as many times today as you can.

85

IN THE SECOND PASSAGE OF THE HEART, compassion is extended to others and to all living things. But it is also extended to you. You, holding compassion for yourself.

When you enter the heart of compassion, you are at the beginning of self love. Write today about how you love yourself!

86

How can you feel compassion for yourself? How can you not?

Close your eyes for a moment and hold compassion for all your sorrows, your regrets, your mistakes, and your shadows. Hold compassion for yourself in the same way you have held compassion for others.

87

The heart of compassion is felt as a softening, an expansion. It is as if the entire heart is flooded with love. And yet, the pain is still there; it has not yet transmuted into pure love. Thus, it is a time of both: the pain ebbing, the compassion flowing.

Write down some incidents where you felt pain. Now close your eyes and allow yourself to bring compassion to these rememberings, these past events.

88

It is difficult at first, to hold compassion for people who victimized you. This can be a task that takes a lifetime. The opening of this particular expansion of the heart is a Divine gift.

Who has hurt you the most deeply? Is it possible for you to have compassion for this person? Why, or why not? Simply consider this idea. Do not attempt to force yourself, one way or the other.

89

It is difficult at first to hold compassion for yourself if you've hurt someone else. There is no sin. You are not perfect. You will make mistakes, and you will learn that you are no different from others who make mistakes.

If you have hurt someone, do you need to make this right in some way? Or do you simply need to release this mistake? Try now to hold compassion for yourself as an imperfect being.

90

In this lifetime you will be hurt, and you will hurt others. This is true for every being, except those few who are saints, the truly ascended who walk on the earth. All humans will be hurt and all will hurt. Accepting this and holding compassion for this is the second passage.

What if you could allow yourself to be free of self-loathing for what you have done, for the mistakes you have made? Consider this today.

91

There is no sin. There are only mistakes made from your particular vibrational state and your particular consciousness. Those lower in consciousness will make bigger and more disturbing mistakes. Those with higher consciousness will also make mistakes, in ways that are just as disturbing to them. Don't expect to be perfect! That isn't why you're here.

Write how you're not perfect. Celebrate this!

92

To be holy does not mean to be mistake free. To be holy does not mean to be perfect. To be holy is to be everything: full integration of your human and diving beings in one body.

Write how you're not integrated—how you still have ideas of "good" and "bad." What might happen if you allowed this integration?

93

There is no forgiveness. That is not a concept that is useful for you. Instead of forgiveness, which contains the energy of having power or control over another, try the idea of compassion.

Today, instead of forgiving another for what you view as a fault, hurt, betrayal, or sin, simply hold this other person in your mind with compassion.

94

People often resist the idea that there is no forgiveness. But the concept of having compassion for another as an equal human being is different from the idea of forgiving, which places one human over another.

Today, someone will cross your path in a negative way. Don't forgive them. Just hold compassion, for them, and for yourself.

95

FORGIVENESS LEADS TO CONTROL, one person better than another; compassion leads to connection, all souls equal, as One, which is the third passage of the heart.

Consider today why forgiveness, or non-forgiveness is an act of control. Consider why compassion is an act of love. Just turn this idea over in your mind.

96

LOOK INTO THE PAST. INSTEAD OF FORGIVING your worst enemy, your worst nemesis, now hold compassion for that person. Instead of accepting that someone has forgiven you, consider that they've held compassion for you.

Think back to those you have forgiven and those who say they've forgiven you. Reframe these relationships with the heart of compassion. Are you beginning to feel the difference?

97

DO YOU NOTICE HOW COMPASSION BRINGS HEALING on an equal plane? Both beings, both entities, accept each other as equal souls.

Write down how you and your worst enemy from the past are equal. If you still can't see this, ask the Divine to illuminate you.

98

COMPASSION FOR YOURSELF becomes easier after the first time you try it. In heart of pain there is a release of grieving. In the heart of compassion, we feel the early shimmering of pure love.

Remember today: compassion is hard to maintain at first, but as you experience it more, compassion becomes a state of being you can easily return to.

99

EVEN A SMALL BIT OF ENERGY CHANGES THINGS. Practice compassion today for five minutes. Turn your compassion on, so to speak, wherever you see it's needed. Don't discriminate. Turn it on for whoever appears.

Do you see how the energy shifts? Do you see how you shift? Do you see how the negative energy dissipates and positive energy fills the gap?

100

THE ABILITY TO HOLD COMPASSION FOR OTHERS is intricately entangled with your ability to hold compassion for yourself. You are not so different from others. In fact, you are not different at all.

Think about this today: the cycle of compassion of other to self, self to other. This a continuous, expanding loop of positive energy.

101

When you are in the practice of holding compassion for another, imagine for a moment that you and this person are the same. You are, you know! This realization opens many things, including you.

Try this: image you are actually another. See if you gain a new sense of this person. Also notice if you begin to receive intuitive information about this person.

102

As we have discussed, some people find it easy to hold compassion for others, but not for themselves: as if they are not worthy. You *are* worthy. Regardless of what you have done or not done, you are worthy of your own compassion.

Think of all your good deeds and all your bad deeds. Imagine your good deeds outweigh the bad. Can you then hold compassion for yourself? What if your bad deeds outweigh the good? Why or why not?

103

This cracking open into the heart of compassion is where many people get stuck. The idea of holding compassion for themselves still eludes them. Don't get stuck! Get awake!

Today, for five minutes, hold deep compassion for yourself. Just five minutes. Even if you consider yourself not good enough or unworthy, allow this Divine healing to touch you.

104

THIS IDEA OF UNWORTHINESS, of sin, of being unsalvageable—it's not true! You took on this idea when you first were hurt, wounded, and knew pain. But it's a misbelief. You don't need it.

Write down all the rotten things you can think of about yourself. Make as long a list as you like. Now, read this list to yourself—and laugh. There's nothing more right or wrong about you than anyone else. We're all both good and bad. This is perfect balance!

105

SOME DAYS YOU FEEL GOOD. Some days you feel bad. Neither is reality. You have the ability to shift emotions; you have the ability to shift vibrations. You can do this as easily as holding intention and using the breath.

You know this! And yet sometimes it feels hard to breathe. The first breath is always the hardest. Take one now. And two more times. Already you have shifted! Already you have raised your vibration!

106

ONE WAY TO FIND COMPASSION for yourself is to go into nature. See how nature loves you, regardless of your so called faults and missteps? You do not have to be perfect for nature to heal you. You do not have to be worthy.

Go into nature, and let the energy heal you. If nature is willing to hold energy for you, what does this tell you? Write about it.

107

SIT AMONG THE TREES. IF YOU DO NOT have trees where you live, sit with the earth, sky, or water. Allow yourself to feel the deep peace nature brings. Allow yourself to take this, as a gift to yourself.

What clarity came to you during this time of respite? What vibration did you notice? Write about it.

108

SELF-LOATHING IS THE ROOT OF ALL ADDICTION, all misery. And it's a construct of the mind; an incorrect construct. It is a misbelief! The truth is this: we are not meant to be perfect. We are only meant to grow.

You've grown more than you can remember. Take a moment and look back one year, three years, and then ten years. See clearly how you have grown. Even when you felt stuck, you were growing.

109

THE PURPOSE OF LIFE IS NOT PERFECTION. The purpose of life is soul growth. As humans, we experience soul growth in the expansion of our hearts through the four passages: pain, compassion, connection, love. This is our journey, here in this lifetime.

If nothing mattered in your life except your soul growth, how would you approach your life? How would you approach your own idea of your self?

110

EVERYTHING THAT IS MATERIAL AMBITION IS FALSE. Nothing matters. You achieve, you amass, and it's just another form of distraction, of addiction. The real truth that matters is how far you can open your heart.

Where are you now in your heart's growth? Are you still in pain? Have you moved to Compassion? Do you think you are already in Connection? Take a moment and feel where you are. There is no right answer. There is only where you are right now.

111

THE OPENING OF THE HUMAN HEART is a life's journey. It may take you twenty years to move from heart of pain into heart of compassion. It may take you twenty seconds.

Where do you think you are in your soul growth? Write down how this feels today.

112

THOSE WHO REMAIN UNCONSCIOUS will not even approach the heart of pain. They will stay numb, stuck, and asleep in this lifetime. Each person takes his or her own path; this is how it works.

Write how it feels to realize that many of those closest to you may remain numb and stuck in their lifetime. Feel this as pain. Then feel it again as compassion.

113

Do not worry about how long any opening takes you. Just focus on where you are and what you are able to experience. Some of you have been born fully conscious; others, are just awakening. We start where we are.

Think of a beautiful younger soul you know, who is more advanced in soul growth than you. Think of an older soul; a soul your age. Write down what these beings teach you.

114

Always, we are presented with people ahead of us on the path of soul growth. Always, we are presented with synchronicities and signs, direct guidance from the Universe that helps us move forward.

What was happening in your life during the times when you moved forward into pain, into compassion. Who helped you to move through these passages? Write down the people who synchronistically arrived in your life at these times.

115

Sometimes when a person is in a state of becoming conscious quickly, the heart will open immediately through all four passages: pain, compassion, connection, and even into love. This is not a miracle. This is just what is possible. This may happen to you.

If you understood that you would be transformed into pure love today, how would this change you?

116

SOMETIMES PEOPLE REFUSE TO BEGIN OPENING the heart because they feel it will be unbearable. It will not. But if you resist change, if you numb yourself to the possibility of opening, the Universe may see fit to assist you. Sometimes this is what must happen.

When were the times the Universe intervened in your life? Recall an illness, accident, separation, divorce, or death that changed you, shifted you, and opened you.

117

THE UNIVERSE MOVES YOU TOWARD SOUL GROWTH, which is your highest possibility. The Universe moves you to your highest possibility, your highest vibration, always.

If you realize the Universe will never participate in anything that lowers your vibration; that a lower vibration is always a human doing, how does this affect how you think of yourself and view your life?

118

THE LAW OF GRAVITY AFFECTS THE BODY of humans on earth. The law of levity rules the Divine nature of humans on earth. Eventually, over time, everything rises: emotions, vibrations, and our essence.

If you understood that you were continually rising, expanding, becoming more etheric, becoming more Divine, how would this affect how you think of yourself and your life?

119

THE LAW OF LEVITY ALWAYS TRUMPS the law of gravity. Vibration always rises to its highest level. This is why saints, the holy ones, the ascended, always have the ability to raise the vibration of those who are around them.

Who in your life automatically causes your vibration to rise? Who in your life do you have trouble holding high vibrations with?

120

VIBRATIONAL MATCHING IS THE PHENOMENON by which you find energetic resonance with another; by which you match the frequency, level, or layer of vibration of another person.

Notice today with whom you are in vibrational match. Who raises your vibration, and with whom do you struggle to hold your own vibration high?

121

WHEN YOU BEGIN TO UNDERSTAND that with each passage of the heart (pain, compassion, connection, and love), you are also raising your vibration and raising consciousness, you begin to understand how the earth emotions and the Divine self are ever intertwined, ever entangled.

Do you see how you are both Earth essence and Divine essence? Look today for ways this is true. Ask the Universe to show you.

122

WHEN YOU UNDERSTAND THAT YOU ARE ONE of One, there is no challenge in raising your vibration to its highest soul level. You simply match frequency to the highest realm of Divine/One/All, of which you are already part. This is simple. This is done through the heart.

Click into the highest vibration you can reach in meditation. Now, imagine your heart opening to contain this vibration. Feel all aspects of yourself seamlessly integrating.

123

BY RAISING YOUR CONSCIOUSNESS through opening the heart, many of the common problems of your culture disappear: anxiety, anger, rage, boredom, ennui, and depression.

How often are you plagued by looping states of mind and obsessions? Notice today when you are fully present and when you are merely looping. Notice when you are actively engaged and when you are obsessed with distraction.

124

THESE LOOPING STATES OF MIND can exist only in lower vibrational states. When you increase vibration by mediation, prayer, exercise, or nature, these states cannot exist.

When you notice your thoughts looping today, simply remind yourself that your vibrational state allows these thoughts to continue. Change your state of vibration and these distractions easily end. Begin this with the breath.

125

YOU MAY CHOOSE LEVITY, or you may choose gravity. Before you are conscious, it's easy to become habituated to the downward pull of gravity; to the state of numbing and shutting down. But once conscious, levity feels better. You enjoy being awake.

Is there a way you can relax in your life without numbing out? Can you relax without drugs, alcohol, addictions, shopping, media, and obsession? Consider how you might do this today.

126

BECOMING CONSCIOUS IS NOT ABOUT gaining control of your emotions. It is about recognizing emotions for what they are: constantly changing states of vibrational being that represent the heart's need to open into light. Emotions are how the body reminds us to expand.

Close your eyes and feel your emotions now, in your body. You may be surprised by where you feel stuck or where you are expanded. This may be different than you think.

127

EMOTIONS ARE PROCESSED OVER TIME. Thus, the feelings you have in your heart as a child may be the same feelings you hold there now. This is true unless your heart has expanded and allowed these feelings to release.

Do you see how past emotions dissipate when they are illuminated in this way, through the heart?

128

ONCE YOU'VE BEEN ABLE TO HOLD OTHERS and self in the heart of compassion, you will begin to feel relief in your life. You will begin to feel free of pain, anger, and lower vibration, as you move into higher consciousness. This is a lovely way to live!

Close your eyes and imagine your heart now unshackled: not all the way, but some. The physical body has parted, the inner armor has released. See this and recognize it.

129

WHEN YOU HAVE COMPASSION FOR OTHERS, when you have compassion for yourself, everything is easy! Everything is simple! There are no storms of anger and no grudges, there is no holding of low vibration. There is no possibility of becoming stuck when you are in this vibration.

Open today! Open! If you not know how to do this, simply close your eyes ask to receive this Divine opening! That is all that it requires; it will happen before you ask.

130

YOU ARE AWARE OF WARS, TORTURE, suffering, and rage. In heart of compassion you see these differently. Instead of being in fear, instead of living in fear, you see them as states of low vibration, low frequency.

You may infuse lower vibration states with higher vibrations. You may do this with your own intention. Call into your mind a situation where suffering is rampant, and then hold the vibration for this situation.

131

YOU SEE YOUR OWN ENERGY AND YOUR own ability to lift others with your thoughts, your actions, and your intention. In this way, those who hold the heart of compassion begin to lift the whole world.

How would you like to lift the whole world today? Simply close your eyes and hold compassion for the whole world. It is simple; yet it is also a miracle.

132

IF YOU ENJOY BEING ACTIVE, DO GOOD WORKS. If you like to be still, do meditation for the world. There are as many ways to lift the world as there are paths to the Divine.

What is your chosen way to lift the world? Do it today.

133

ONCE YOU ARE LIVING IN HEART OF COMPASSION, you may feel your life begin to change and shift. How can it not? When your vibration lifts, when you vibration rises, everything becomes easier, happier, and more fulfilling.

Write about three ways your life has changed since you began this course, and since you moved from heart of pain into heart of compassion.

134

WHEN YOU MOVE OUT OF THE ME, my, and mine ego state, you allow room for a state of compassion for all humans on the planet, for your own existence on the planet, and for the existence of every sentient being on the planet. This is a beautiful way to live!

Consider today the trees, plants, animals, and fish; all living and sentient things. Hold compassion today for all of these.

135

TAKE A MOMENT TODAY AND NOTICE a situation that once might have triggered you to feel anxious and unsure. Do you see how, when you are living in the heart of compassion, these states are not possible?

Today, hold the heart of compassion immediately after a time when you feel bothered by someone, or something. Do you notice, once again, how quickly things shift when you move into this vibration?

136

YOU HAVE MOVED QUICKLY FROM HEART of pain to heart of compassion. Enjoy this new state! Watch in amazement as your life shifts and transforms, so that what was low vibration dissolves away, and what is high vibration seems to greet you at every turn.

Rejoice! You may expect more of this today; you may expect more of this forever.

137

ONCE YOU HAVE GONE THROUGH these two particular doors, pain and compassion, you will never go back there again. It is a one-way process, from darkness to light.

What does this mean to you, that you will never go back? How does this make you feel? This is how you will begin to feel all the time.

138

IF THE ENTIRE WORLD COULD EXIST in the heart of compassion, all the world's problems would be solved. However, there is no time in your lifetime when the world will reach this vibrational level. If you are conscious now, you are early to the game.

Understand that you are a pioneer, and that the world may not follow your path in your lifetime. Does this make you feel hopeless, or hopeful?

139

AS YOU MASTER THE HEART OF COMPASSION, you will begin moving in this vibration continually and with ease. It will be the most natural state for you; the vibration you naturally access as your response to a situation. You will begin feeling better and better at all times.

When compassion has become your first response to situations, notice how the old ideas of temper, discomfort, fear, and hurt have dissipated and are no longer at the front of your awareness.

140

WHEN COMPASSION INSTEAD OF PAIN is your first response, you will notice your body feels different. In pain, you feel constricted, shut down, numb, raw, and tight. In compassion you feel a softening of the body: a releasing in the heart.

Close your eyes and notice any areas of contraction. Allow yourself to expand in those places. Whenever you slip out of this state, simply breathe, and then reenter it again.

141

AFTER YOU HAVE BEEN IN THE HEART of compassion long enough: for a day, a month, a year, or a decade, you will notice your heart beginning to open further. Here you will begin opening into the heart of connection. At this time you will experience a spiritual awakening.

Write down if you feel you are ready for a spiritual awakening now, or if you need more time. Also, write down if you are impatient for this to happen.

142

THE HEART OF CONNECTION MAY ARRIVE to you early, or it may arrive late. Always, it comes at the absolutely perfect time.

Do you feel impatient about your spiritual awakening? Write down what arrives to you. Then, release this need to control time, outcome, and opening. Also release any ideas of what this might look like.

143

THE HEART OF CONNECTION IS THE GIFT of consciousness. When you have walked through this door you enter into a new universe of conscious creation, of mysticism as reality, of intuitive opening, of joy.

If you feel you've already reached this state, recall the day and moment this happened for you. If you feel you have not yet reached this state, ask your heart when it will be ready.

144

As CONSCIOUSNESS INCREASES, time begins to swirl in a new way. You may feel time has sped up, or your perception of it has changed. You experience boredom less often; you experience being stuck in low vibration less often. Instead of the scrambled, panicked feeling you felt about time in the past, now you feel a sense of deep relaxation.

Write down how you feel about schedules, time, hurrying, and pacing. Where are you on this continuum now?

145

EVEN A SHORT TIME AGO you were controlled by your schedule and "to do" list. Now, as you enter into heart of connection, you realize that time, also, is one of One. There is no difference in all the layers and levels of the Universe: time, space, matter, and you.

Check in now and see what emotions emerge surrounding your "to do" list. What differences do you notice?

146

THE LAST FEW YEARS HAVE BROUGHT a clearing and decluttering. You have seen this globally as changes on the planet remove excess and imbalance. You have also seen this in your own life.

How have you been asked to release ideas, things, and relationships? Write about this.

147

ENERGETICALLY, THIS TIME IS SIMILAR to a great housecleaning in the spring; all the excessive items and objects are taken away, the windows are flung open, and the fresh breeze blows in. This is the place you are in now.

What else needs to be cleared or cleaned? Ask your heart, today.

148

CLEARING OR CLEANING MAY BE IN A PLACE at your home or place of work. It may be in your body. It may be energetic, in releasing emotions and energies that are no longer useful to you.

Look today at what may still need releasing. Notice if you feel resistance at this letting go. Ask your heart why.

149

THE BODY IS A CONTAINER FOR THE SOUL; yet it also is an energetic Universe. Without support in the form of nutrition, exercise, sleep, and touch, the body cannot thrive as a Universe.

In what ways do you protect your body and heal your body? What is your body calling for you to do today? In what ways do you obsess on your body? Is this required by you?

150

THE PLEASURES OF THE BODY are manifold. Many of you are diligent in the pursuit of health, vibrancy, and performance. But when the focus is only on the body—when the body is used as a releasing point instead of using the heart—this is not useful.

Do you exercise to feel good? What happens if you do not exercise on a given day? Where do the feelings that need to be released go, then?

151

IF YOU ARE EXERCISING TO RELEASE your feelings, to have the adrenaline rush serve as your method of clearing your emotions, this is like running from a bear. Better to sit and engage the monster than run away from it.

If you have a regular practice of movement or exercise, consider how you are using this practice. If you use it as a method of release without consciousness, please consider that this is a false releasing.

152

THERE IS A DIFFERENT RELEASE in exercise or in physicality than when you release from the heart. The physical release is temporary. The heart release is energetic, and infinite.

Today, allow all the rage, fear, and pain in your heart to come forward, as it does when you begin to move. This time, release that energy directly from your heart. You will feel a difference, energetically. You will release the pain energetically, not just physically.

153

FOR THOSE WHO DO NOT USE THE BODY, you are neglecting a marvelous gift! The body is pleasure, with every step, breath, turn, and twist. The body is pleasure as you walk, eat, and touch. This container of the senses is provided to you as a gift.

If you have not exercised for a long time, do so now. Get up and simply stretch, like a cat awakening from a long nap. The pleasure of your body is yours at every moment. Today, find ways to enjoy this gift.

154

THE MODERN LIFESTYLE IS NOT DESIGNED for movement. It is designed to hold the body still and to have the mind work—not in the realms of love and delight, but in the realms of information.

Notice today how often you are immersed in the computer, reading, talking on the phone, and so on. These are times when your brain works, but your body is still. Attempt to take one hour out of this day and simply lie on the floor and stretch, or take a walk, or bathe. Be in your body, not your mind.

155

THE BODY IS SACRED, THE BODY IS REVERENT, the body is Divine. There is no time this is not true.

Today, celebrate your body, no matter what condition you find yours in. Celebrate it as a miracle.

156

IF YOU ARE OUT OF BALANCE WITH YOUR BODY: overweight, poor nutrition, or addictions, ask yourself why. Ask your heart to show you the memories, situations, or pain that may have started you on this path.

Being out of balance is not about the food or substances you eat. It is about the emotions you have not accessed or released. Think of your body and then write down what emotions come up for you. If you are ready, release them.

157

WHEN WAS THE LAST TIME YOU FELT TRULY GOOD in your body? The body is an energetic Universe manifested in physical form. As you provide the body with nutrition, movement, and sleep, your body vibrates at a higher level. Similarly, as you exist in higher vibration your body is also healed.

Close your eyes and first ask your body what it needs. Then ask your heart what it needs. Ask the Divine to provide you with clear guidance on this balance, today.

158

CONSIDER THE BALANCE IN YOUR OWN BODY: first, the physical care you provide to yourself, and then the emotional care you provide. One does not replace the other. Both must be in evidence to reach true vibration and vitality.

Today, write a list of what you to do keep your body healthy. Next, write a list of what you do to keep your emotions healthy. Notice if one list is longer than the other.

159

EMOTIONAL ENERGY DETERMINES VITALITY. Balancing your emotional energy includes meditating, prayer, talk, touch, and sex, as well as any time you are basking in the bliss of being cared for by yourself, or by others.

Do you provide yourself with ongoing emotional support? Today, look at areas where you support others, and where you allow yourself to be supported. Is this in balance?

160

RAISING VIBRATION IN THE PHYSICAL BODY is achieved through nutrition, movement, sleep, and touch. And yet, in reality, your vibration is only partly determined through the body. There is more to the equation than physicality.

Do you have the habits of optimum health, or do you not? If you don't, do you feel guilty about this? If you do practice these habits, do you feel superior about it? Examine your ideas about your physical body.

161

RAISING VIBRATION IN THE EMOTIONAL BODY is achieved through meditation, prayer, talk, connection, touch, sex, and nature. These are all profound practices. And these practices are symbiotic—both are required: high vibration in the body, and high vibration in emotions.

Consider your spiritual practice. Consider your physical practice. Is one lacking? Is one overly pronounced? Seek balance today.

162

RAISING VIBRATION IS SHIFTING CONSCIOUSNESS. Shifting your consciousness results in opening the heart into pure joy, love, and bliss. This is possible for you in this lifetime! It is possible for anyone.

Are you ready to raise your vibration and shift consciousness? Ask the Divine to assist you today. Write down what happens.

163

THE BODY IS BOTH A CONTAINER AND AN ESSENCE; it is both physical and emotional, a skeleton and a soul. When you raise or lower the vibration in one aspect, the other aspect is also raised or lowered. One affects the other, in synergy.

Close your eyes and allow your mind to return to the first time you raised your vibration today. See if you can do this again, and again, today.

164

CONSIDER THE VIBRATION OF A HUMMINGBIRD, of a human, and of a stone. Each varies in frequency. Even in the same categories, such as human to human, one person may vibrate higher or lower than another on any given day, in a given moment.

Where is your vibration today? Imagine a small sliding bar in your mind's eye, with low vibration on the left, and high vibration on the right. Hold a vision of this bar in your mind and allow it to slide to wherever it pleases: to the left, then to the right, then somewhere in between. Notice where it ends. Let this inform you today.

165

ENERGY VIBRATES AT A FREQUENCY. This is the same thing, using different words, as saying that consciousness unfolds.

How has your consciousness unfolded since you began this course. What shifts have you noticed? How has your energy shifted in vibration?

166

THERE ARE MANY OTHER WAYS TO DISCUSS THE INEFFABLE; choose whatever story, metaphor, parable, science, or example is right for you. There is no incorrect path to the Divine.

Tell yourself a story today about your own expanding, unfolding consciousness. If you cannot find your story in your own mind, allow the Divine you to provide you with this story today, in some way.

167

WE ARE ONE WITH ONE OF ALL UNIVERSAL ENERGY, but as humans, we aren't able to grasp the scope of this in our minds. It's too much. The closest we can get is bliss. Thus, we use the story, the metaphor, the small slice of a particular experience to help us understand.

The Universe continually provides these small slices of information for you to use. Notice one today.

168

SIGNS AND SYNCHRONICITIES ABOUND. You don't even have to look for them. They will appear, unbidden, if you are open. They are hard to miss unless you are asleep. Wake up! Notice! The Universe is communicating with you even now.

For the next hour, watch for signs and synchronicities to appear. Be amazed by how quickly this happens.

169

WHEN YOU FIRST BEGIN RAISING YOUR VIBRATION through your practices and habits, you will notice a great deal of shifting. This may happen in the physical body, such as soreness, discomfort, and even illness as the body reaches a new stasis. Or it may happen in the emotional body as the emotions swirl into a new balance.

How do you feel today? Better or worse than usual? Different? You cannot feel the same, for each day is a new Universe of energy. Write how you feel.

170

WHEN YOU DO A CLEANSE, you take away from the body the distractions it has known: the addictions, chemicals, and toxins you used to shift the body into a different way of feeling.

If it feels right, limit what goes into your body today. Notice how you feel.

171

WHEN YOU RELEASE EMOTIONS you have felt for a long period of time, the effect is at first the same: disorientation, discomfort, and a sense that all is lost.

If it feels right, release some emotions you have been holding for a while. Simply ask to release them and this will happen for you today. If you feel discomfort, hold on as this feeling dissipates.

172

FOOD, ALCOHOL, AND DRUGS ARE TOXINS; but toxins may also include excessive exercise, lack of sleep, and other physical addictions of trying to be too "good" or "pure."

Ask your body today what it needs for balance. Skip the "shoulds" that may arrive first. Look deeper. What is your body calling for? Rest? A break? Sleep?

173

IT IS NOT NORMAL OR NECESSARY FOR THE BODY to be pure at all times. This is a misbelief. Even for optimum health, this is not required. The body is of the earth, and the body's highest function is to be able to process what the earth life provides.

Are you too strict with your diet or health? Are you not strict at all? How does this aspect serve you? How is it merely another attachment, distraction, or trap?

174

THE PERSON WHO IS HUNGRY does not worry what food he eats; the desire is to fill the belly. The person who lives in such abundance that he can obsess over the food he eats—that is a different story.

When was the last time you were really, truly hungry? How did this inform you? If you have not been hungry in a long time, how might hunger be useful for you?

175

THE PERSON WHO IS SATED, who is overly full, is also like a starving person; nothing that fills the mouth will ever satisfy.

Do the foods you eat satisfy you, or are they merely habit? Look at this today.

176

THE PERSON WHO IS OVER-SATED stuffs him or herself in an attempt to feel more. The person who overindulges keeps trying to eat, drink, use drugs, or smoke more—but after a certain point it does not satisfy.

When you eat, drink, smoke, use drugs or take medications today, notice the feeling of relief this brings. Don't judge it. Just notice.

177

THE PHYSICAL BODY CANNOT BE SATED BY FOOD, drink, alcohol, and so forth, because the physical body cannot answer conditions of the emotional body. This is like trying to feed an apple to a stone; stone's cannot eat apples. Apples do not nourish them.

What feeds you emotionally? What doesn't? Make a list of these things and place the list where you can see it the next few days. Notice how the list is different than you expected.

178

THE BODY IS NOT MEANT ONLY FOR FASTING, deprivation, and the dry and tasteless experiences of a renunciate. That is only one path. The body is also meant for pure pleasure and reckless abandon—the full filling up, the feast. This is another path. Both paths are useful.

Today, allow yourself to hold the idea of the feast. Feast and celebrate, if you wish. How much feasting do you need in order to be whole? How much fasting?

179

THE FEAST IS OF GREAT USE for the emotional body. The celebration, the indulgence, the enjoyment and vigor of emotions allows you to feel more. This is useful for you.

How can you feast today, in your body and in your emotions?

180

THE PHYSICAL BODY HAS A METHOD for continually cleansing itself through the pores and digestive system. Even the blood is regularly cleansed. The emotional body does not have his system. Thus, you must provide this for yourself with regular moments of meditation, prayer, movement, talk, connection, and sex.

In what ways do you clean and clear your emotional body? Write down some daily methods you use to release your emotions.

181

THE PHYSICAL BODY CAN CHANGE in an instant, but mostly it changes slowly. You eat a meal and feel one way. You sleep and feel another way. The emotional body can change in milliseconds, riding up one wave of emotion and down the other. The waves are not true: they are just the movement of energy, up or down.

What method do you have for rebalancing yourself when your emotions rise or lower to a point that is not useful for you? Hint: just breathe.

182

IT'S EASY TO MOVE INTO BLISS when you feel bad. However, this does not solve the problem unless you have first moved from pain into compassion. Bliss is a drug if you have not yet moved forward in your heart.

Have you used meditation, running, yoga, sex, and breath to move into bliss when you have been upset? Do you see how this can also be an addiction, a drug, and a trap?

183

WHEN YOU ARE UPSET, you must first release what is in the heart. In this way, you achieve true clearing. The other method—simply moving into the vibration of bliss—is only a temporary fix.

Consider this, today.

184

WHEN YOU ARE UPSET TODAY, let your heart open fully into the heart of pain, the heart of compassion. And once again see what is there. After you have processed the hurt, move into bliss. In this way you will truly be released.

There are two places to release emotions: when you are quiet, still, and alone. And also, when you are surrounded by other beings, in the hubbub. Both are valid.

185

MEDITATE TODAY FOR A FEW MOMENTS by yourself. Enjoy this sense of yourself away from the energy of the world. Also go into a noisy group setting and allow yourself to merge with the energy there. Both are useful.

Notice how you feel when you are by yourself, in quiet. And when you are in a crowd, in noise and chaos. Begin to experiment; to discover how you can retain the quiet in the noise. How you can also choose the noise, in the quiet. Experiment with this today.

186

UNDERSTAND WHO YOU ARE AS A BEING. You are most certainly not the façade, the image, the brand you present to the world. This aspect could be gone in a second; it means nothing.

Feel your deeper self, underneath the image you present to the world. You will not love the façade; it is not real. Your deeper self is your true love.

187

DO YOU KNOW YOUR TRUE SELF? This is the self you knew as a child at age three or five, or eleven. This is your true self, before you began the process of forgetting who you really are.

Ask today, to feel this authentic self moving inside of you. See how this is different than your façade.

188

IN THIS WORLD OF ELECTRONICA, the façade is what is seen and heard. It is only the rarest person who dares reveal his or her true self on electronica.

Consider your usage of electronica and social media. This is a way of connecting, yes. But it is also a way of connecting that which is not true. Is this useful to you?

189

ELECTRONICA IS THE NEWEST ADDICTION; it has replaced consumerism, the desire for material things. This is a new aspect to arrive in human evolution and it has quickly shifted things.

How many times do you use electronica each day? Does it make your life better or worse? How do you feel when you spend a day, a week, or a month without being connected to this group energy?

190

THE GROUP ENERGY IN ELECTRONICA leads to group thought and is a way of connecting you more deeply to those with whom you feel in alignment. When you cluster with those you feel similar to, you begin to identify more fully with the group. In this situation you may find it hard to resist group thought.

How have you been affected by group thought in the last week? The last day? Notice this today when you are on electronica. Notice whether or not you are your true self.

191

THE EXPERIENCE OF GROUP THOUGHT on electronica may feel uncomfortable. Do you feel separate, rebellious, angry, or dismayed? How does this energy feel differently than when you are with another person, one on one?

Do you feel you are not your true self when you are on electronica? Do you notice the difficulty in unplugging, in pulling away? If you take a break for a day or a week, do you notice you feel better?

192

GROUP THOUGHT CAN BE A MEANS OF RAISING the vibration of collective soul. As you know from history, it can also be a means of lowering the vibration.

Use caution in all group thought, in all cult thought. Understand that electronica creates cults. Know your own mind.

193

HOW DOES GROUP THOUGHT create cult thought? It is useful to understand that electronica is both a tool for Divine and a tool for fear.

When you are on electronica today, notice what you agree with and then ask yourself, "Is this really true? Is it absolutely true, or is it just group thought that has captured me?"

194

THE ABILITY TO KNOW YOUR OWN MIND is the true sign of consciousness. In consciousness, in awakening you see that all thoughts scatter about a circle, with the more extreme thoughts on each side of the circle. In consciousness you are able to stay in the middle.

What do you really, truly believe? Name five things you are absolutely sure of. Now, take a deep breath and look with detachment at these beliefs. Are they still true? In what way is it possible that they are not?

195

WHEN YOU ARGUE WITH SOMEONE, look outside the "facts" of the matter. Instead, consider vibration, frequency, and energy. Instead of arguing facts, move into heart of compassion and match vibrations. This does not mean lowering your vibration—what will happen is, the other person will rise to your higher vibration when you hold it there.

Every time you feel like arguing with someone today, match vibration instead. Simply raise your vibration and invite them telepathically to match it. This shift may surprise you with its effectiveness and ability to create change.

196

WHEN YOU UNDERSTAND how little is "true," you move toward conscious awakening. Again, recall the circle: the thoughts and beliefs and attachments that may seem most real, most compelling to you, are actually on the outer part of the circle. The inner point of balance and detachment is where real truth resides—in the middle.

What's true? What isn't true? What's important? What isn't important? Things are much less clear than you might imagine. Begin to examine what you've been told and taught, and then see if it is correct, for you.

197

FROM THE BEGINNING WE ARE RAISED in group thought. The family directs use one way, our schools direct us, and so do our jobs, friends, and activities. When you immerse yourself in a different cult by traveling, changing your identity, and all the other ways this can happen, you broaden your viewpoint. You move away from group thought toward the center of the circle.

When in your lifetime have you existed outside your particular cult, group, tribe, or corporation? Today, seek an opportunity to do this, even in a small way.

198

IF YOU DON'T FEEL YOU KNOW YOUR OWN MIND or identity outside of your group, do not be dismayed. Detachment from group mind in the lower vibrations takes time. And, in the end, you will evolve to be part of a group mind at the highest vibration you can manage. This is your journey: Escape from group mind in the lower vibration and connect to group mind as One/All/Divine at the highest vibration.

What would it mean for you to disconnect from group thought, cult thought—all the people and energy conglomerates that tell you who you are? What are you left with if you disconnect? Is this frightening, or exhilarating?

199

THE ABILITY TO HOLD YOUR OWN THOUGHTS while in group energy; to retain high vibrations while surrounded by low vibrations; this is something you may learn. When you speak of "protection" or "boundaries," this is misbelief. In truth, it is all about holding a high vibration.

Today, go into a situation where you expect vibrations to be low. Do not use protection; do not set boundaries. Instead, simply hold your vibration at the highest level you can and exist at that frequency for as long as you can.

200

GROUP THOUGHT, WHEN IT MOVES INTO FEAR, is one of the most difficult vibrations to avoid. You feel it around you in the very air and on your skin. This happens even if you live in isolation; you still feel the vibration. If you are in a crowded city, you feel everything.

Understand how group thought, group fear, and group panic affects you. Understand your need to continually clear and raise your energy from this lower vibration of group thought.

201

JESUS SAID, "WHEREVER TWO OR THREE of you are gathered in my name, there is love." If you have trouble holding a high vibration on your own, find one or two others to do this with you.

If you are not able to hold high vibrations on your own, seek one or two others who can help. If you can hold this vibration on your own, help others. This small encounter may be like nothing you have imagined.

202

HOLDING CONSCIOUSNESS IS LIKE holding a small, bright lantern into the dark recesses of the world. The world is for the most part a sea of unconsciousness. At this time, however, a small percentage of you are gaining consciousness. This small bit of light may not change the world, but it will change the lives of those who are illuminated.

How have you become illuminated in the last few months? Write down ways your consciousness has expanded.

203

UNDERSTAND THAT IN THIS LIFETIME not everyone seeks, and not everyone will find. Most are still sleeping; this has always been so. At any given time only a few are illuminated.

You, reading this, are seeking. You, reading this, will find. Shine your light today and help others who may be ready to become illuminated.

204

TO BE ILLUMINATED DOES NOT MEAN "BETTER." You can only be where you are. To be illuminated, to be conscious, to be able to see and understand and work with energy, only means you have moved through the heart of pain and through the heart of compassion. There are more passages to come! This opening is just the beginning.

As a person who has been through the heart of pain and the heart of compassion, how has this changed you? Do you lend a hand to those who are on their way through these passages? Today, see if there is an opportunity for you to do so.

205

THE MOST ELEVATED BEINGS ON EARTH, the saints and holy ones, are there to lift us up, to help us, show by example, and be models for our aspirations. The lowliest ones on earth are there for us to help in the ways we can.

You are in the middle: being helped, and helping. Find an opportunity to do both today.

206

WHO CAN YOU HELP WITHOUT FEAR? Who do you still need to avoid helping because they are too toxic for you? Who are you unable to help? This may often be those you are closest to. Each person walks his or her own soul path. We may only be helped if we ask; we may only help if we are asked.

Determine today who surrounds you and if you are to help them or simply witness them.

207

THE WITNESSING OF ANOTHER SOUL in struggle; the person you cannot help, the person on his or her own path that you cannot help no matter what—there is grace in this. Holding witness, holding this other person in your deepest heart of compassion, is a gift of energy and love.

Make a list of those you have tried to help, fix, or solve things for —but your efforts for these people were not effective. Today, simply hold these people in your heart of compassion and wish them well. This is a blessing.

208

IT IS NOT YOUR JOB TO FIX OR CHANGE OTHERS. Each person is on his or her particular path of soul growth. You may advise, you may direct from a place of higher wisdom or knowing; but the ultimate choice lies with that person. Each person must come to consciousness—or not—in his or her own time.

Today, release your worries about those you have tried to help those you have tried to advise. Trust that soul growth happens in each lifetime at the speed it needs to happen.

209

WHAT APPEARS TO BE FAILURE may merely be a processing through the heart of pain. This is the first passage and is to be applauded. When you see failure in another, look deeper.

Who in your life is presenting as a "failure?" Look again at this person and notice if they are asleep, or if they are moving into heart of pain.

210

YOU MAY SEE PEOPLE WHO ARE COMFORTABLE in their earth bodies: fit, and healthy. You may see people who are riddled with pain, illness, and disease. Don't be quick to judge the soul inside each body. Understand that the body is merely a container.

What does it mean to have a beautiful body? What does it mean to have a body that is not considered attractive? Consider this today.

211

THE BODY'S HEALTH MAY BE A REFLECTION of emotional health inside, or it may not. The body's illness may be a challenge that allows the soul to grow.

Consider how the Universe has communicated to you in your body. Ask for further direction today.

212

DISEASE, IS DIS-EASE IN PHYSICAL BODY. This dis-ease may act as a pebble in the shoe of the soul, asking the soul to look further into heart of pain, move more gracefully into heart of compassion. Dis-ease invites exploration and expansion until ease is felt.

What does your body invite you to look into more deeply? This does not mean fitness, stamina, or health. It means where is there dis-ease in your body? How does this inform you?

213

WORRYING ABOUT SCARCITY is a part of human instinct, going back to the beginning of your species when there was not always enough. The fear of being without drove you to find ways to have enough.

What is enough? Is it to be fed and have water and shelter? Is it having material objects, savings, and investments? What is enough to you?

214

YOU FEEL THE ENERGY OF SCARCITY even if you are in abundance. You feel this because you feel everything in the Universe as vibration. What affects the one, affects the One.

How do you deal with the truth that there are many in this world who do not have enough?

215

SCARCITY DOES EXIST IN MANY PARTS of the world. But scarcity thoughts in parts of the world where there is extreme abundance is a construct of group thought, group fear, and group misbelief.

How do you detach from this energy? How do you see your own situation, your place in the world? Do you recognize that you are blessed?

216

MANY OF YOU WILL BE ABLE TO TRAVEL in this lifetime. This is a gift. If you can travel, do so—it is a broadening of perspective. If you cannot travel in your body, do so in your mind. See other parts of the world.

Do you understand how abundance has been bestowed on you with your home, clothing, food, and entertainment? See this clearly. Drop away from group fear, from group thoughts of scarcity.

217

IN THIS WORLD WE THINK IF WE HAVE MORE, we will be happy. Yet this is not true. When you move from heart of pain into heart of compassion, this belief no longer holds and is released. It is no longer possible to hold this belief.

Consider how this belief is no longer part of your thoughts: that more is better. Ask yourself what is required to be happy.

218

FOR MOST OF YOU, LESS MAY ACTUALLY BE BETTER. Less distraction. Less stress. Less clutter of space and mind. Less brings a freedom that is a wild and exhilarating experience. Less allows you to live without fear.

Do you need to live differently? Do you need less? How does this set you free?

219

WHEN THINGS ARE DESTROYED in a natural disaster, the shock of change is overwhelming. This shock, like an electrical current to the heart, often jumps people directly from heart of pain into heart of compassion.

It is easier to make a shift on your own. But sometimes, nature will do this for you. Write of a time when this happened to you. If it has not happened to you, why do you think this is so?

220

MANY OF YOU HAVE HAD TO REBUILD from scratch. This process is an extraordinary opening: the initial numbness and disbelief, the pain, the agony, and finally, the deep sense of deciding to live—the deep sense of deciding to rebuild.

Were there times when you lost everything, including your property, relationships, health, and finances? Remember when you decided to rebuild. How does this inform you today?

221

NATURE IS NEUTRAL. IT IS UNIVERSAL ENERGY as it constantly moves through the infinite cycle of creation and destruction. As a human, you know this in your core. We are of nature, and our bodies are here for the time we are here. Our consciousness knows no such timeline.

Look at the multiple cycles of creation and destruction around you; all the cycles of death and rebirth. Write about some of them you notice today.

222

YOU HAVE TRANSITIONED FROM YOUR most recent past life into this one, through the gateway of death and rebirth. Consciousness never dies; it is universal energy, shifting into a new form. You will also transition someday into another new life during this endless continuum of consciousness known as soul.

Would you like to know what you experienced in a past life? This is not difficult to find. Go into meditation today and ask to be shown. Allow the information and images to come, without censoring them. Be informed by whatever happens.

223

YOUR SOUL WANTS THIS LIFETIME because it needs this experience to expand. It uses this earth life to experience the four passages of the heart—to go as far as it can. Your soul is loving this life experience and where you are. Your soul feels no struggle, only movement and expansion in soul growth.

Wherever you are today is perfect. Take a deep breath, in through the nose and out through the mouth, and allow yourself to understand this fully.

224

EVERYTHING IS EXPERIENCE: soul growth expressed through the human body, expanded in the four passages of the human heart. You will notice we have only spoken of heart of pain and heart of compassion at this point. The other two are arriving soon, for you to begin to experience.

Take a look at all the chaos or perceived chaos around you: all the swirling elements in the world. Ask yourself if you really need to fall into fear, or if there is another way. What if the way was in your heart's opening?

225

THE ONLY PROTECTION YOU HAVE, the only balm, the only healing, is to move from heart of pain to heart of compassion, and into heart of connection. Here is where spiritual awakening fully happens.

Nothing else can save you, protect you, and make you feel secure in this earthly life, save this transition. Today, do you feel ready to make this leap? Why or why not?

226

WE THINK WE CAN CONTROL. We think we can manage. We flail about, trying to control, in hopes this will bring peace. Yet the only way to experience this deep feeling of safety, trust, and peace is to open and expand.

How does this make you feel? How will it feel to let go of control and to surrender? Do you feel ready to do this? If not, why not?

227

THE HEART OF CONNECTION happens when you begin to understand yourself as one of the One. In other words, you are not separate. Many of you say you understand this, but you have not yet felt it. In heart of connection you will open to a place where you can feel this.

Go into meditation and draw every soul in proximity into your heart of compassion. Now expand further. Begin to draw in every person in your building, in your area, in your city, in your country—allow yourself to draw in each person, each soul, without censoring or fear of pain. Allow yourself to feel how each is one of One, as are you.

228

HOW ARE YOU ONE? IT IS SO SIMPLE! At your core you are a universe of particulate energy; at each person's core, this is so. Do you see how this energy is all the same; how you are each made up of the same particulate energy, which is love?

Today, notice the differences between you and another. Now, also notice that you are created from same essence. You know this already—but know it anew.

229

WHEN YOU ARE BEGINNING TO OPEN into the heart of connection, you move beyond compassion for your brother, mother, lover, and other, and you realize you are the same. You realize your particular energy is not only of the same essence, it is the same.

Close your eyes, breathe into relaxation, and hold the idea that you are one of One in your mind. What thoughts arrive to you? Is there resistance? Is there peace?

230

YOUR AURA, YOUR ENERGETIC or subtle body, is expansive. This is true of everyone else on earth. You can see clearly where another's aura merges into yours. At a certain point, even if you are holding your aura close to your body, there is a place where one does not end and another does not begin.

Today, allow your aura to merge, dance, and play with everyone and everything. Do not worry about boundaries for all of today. Just exist, in full energy expansion.

231

WHEN YOU THINK YOU ARE SEPARATE, this is misbelief. It's tempting! It seems easier, at times, to retreat again into that hollow shell of pain. But don't be fooled! Nothing is there for you.

Today, imagine yourself as separate, then as One. Separate, then as One. Do you see how being separate is an illusion?

232

AFTER YOU HAVE BEEN THROUGH HEART OF PAIN and heart of compassion and are moving into heart of connection, it is difficult to retreat, descend, and go back to where you began. You are permanently transformed by the heart's opening. Going back is not only boring; it doesn't offer what you need.

Today, allow yourself to slip into heart of pain for a few moments. Do you see how you are past this point now? You are moving from compassion to connection.

233

THE TIMES WE MOST EASILY FIND OURSELVES as one of One are in times of great heart opening, such as the tantra of sex, birthing a baby, helping someone die, or helping someone in tragedy. These are all times our hearts crack open, without fear.

Recall a time you felt opened beyond yourself. Think about this incident or experience in detail.

234

OPENING INTO THE HEART OF CONNECTION always brings a spiritual awakening. Spiritual awakening is no big thing! It is just what happens when you begin to understand your life from the paradigm of One.

Have you had a spiritual awakening yet? What was it like? Do you want to have one?

235

FOR SOME PEOPLE, SPIRITUAL AWAKENING is overwhelming and the cracking open into heart of connection is a shift that takes years to integrate. For others, it is as simple as one day not yet open to this stage, the next day open; much like a flower unfolding into the light.

How has your heart unfolded this past year? How have you been moving beyond compassion during this last month?

236

THE HEART OF CONNECTION, of knowing oneself as one of One, opens easily in sex. This is because sex is the Divine union of physical, a Divine union of energies. This is the purpose of sex: Oneness.

Do you feel Oneness in sex? If not, why not? What is holding you back?

237

SEX, AS TANTRA, HAS BEEN MISUNDERSTOOD by many of you. It is not technique, position, or even breathing. It is allowing yourself to experience Oneness with another.

Is sex complete for you? Are you seeking Oneness or something else?

238

YOU MAY NOT EXPERIENCE ONENESS with everyone at first; you may only be able to experience Oneness, heart of connection, with a few in the beginning. This is a first step. It is a start. Sometimes Oneness is easier with those you know well. Sometimes it is easier with strangers.

Recall a time when you felt fully connected to a group of people you did not know well. What was happening in this incident or experience?

239

SEX, BIRTH, DISASTER, AND DEATH: these are all peak experiences when you know you're truly alive. These are times when heart of connection opens and you expand beyond yourself, into One.

When was the last time you felt fully, completely alive? What would it take for you feel that way today?

240

AFTER A PEAK EXPERIENCE in which your heart cracks open into connection, in which you understand yourself as One, other openings also occur: spiritual, intuitive, and energetic. This may take time to integrate.

If you have had a peak experience, what happened? If you have not had one, why do you think you have not?

241

ONENESS, OR HEART OF CONNECTION, is not the furthest the heart can be opened. But at this point of expansion your life begins to change dramatically, profoundly, and radically.

If you knew your life would be altered when you realized Oneness, would you still change?

242

ONE OF THE MOST COMMON RESULTS of Oneness, of opening into heart of connection, is that everything unimportant, unreal, and surface level, falls away. This may mean jobs, relationships, and more.

Are your relationships at the level of connection you wish to have? Is your life's work at a level that makes you happy and content?

243

ONCE YOU REACH HEART OF CONNECTION, everything not in alignment with Oneness falls away; it doesn't matter to you anymore. This shedding of the old can be painful, but is the only direction you can go.

Has there been a time in your life when you let everything go? Are there aspects of your life you would be served by letting go of, now?

244

HEART OF CONNECTION is one of the most difficult passages: it is about releasing all the ideas you have been taught since childhood and coming into your own as a conscious adult for the first time. This may happen at age 20, age 40, age 50, or older. There is no age, only readiness.

What beliefs are you following that are no longer yours?

245

HEART OF CONNECTION, ONENESS, does not imply morality, being helpful, or being "good." Instead, it shows you that you are One with all others. Morality isn't part of this view.

Are you ready to drop the misbelief that you must be "good?"

246

A ROCK IS NOT GOOD, A TREE IS NOT GOOD: and yet these are one of One right now, without doing anything. Understand this and let the rest drop away.

Sit with a rock today; sit with a tree. At your essence, you are the same. Energetically there is no difference, except perhaps in vibration.

247

YOUR EXPERIENCES ON THIS EARTH are going to be "good" and "bad," and yet in all cases and situations, you will still be perfectly, absolutely One. No matter what you do, or don't do, this is your existence.

How do you feel about this? Can you let go of the ego's need to be more than One?

248

IT CAN BE HARDER TO OPEN into Oneness with people you know, your family and friends. Why is this? When we think we "know" someone, we know nothing. Each person has the same, equal ability to open into heart of connection and have a spiritual awakening.

Which of your relationships feel the most controlling, trapped, and debilitating to you. What if you knew the person you are in relationship with would have a spiritual awakening today?

249

A SPIRITUAL AWAKENING IS NOT FIRE and brimstone, or angelic heralds. It is simply opening into the understanding of our true nature, our true purpose in this lifetime. It is an understanding that everyone else has also signed up for the same job.

Soul growth happens at different stages for different people. Where are you today in terms of your heart's opening?

250

ALL THE MEDITATION, ALL THE YOGA, all the renunciation in the world will not allow you to reach spiritual awakening. It happens in the heart. That's the only way to get there; nothing else can do it for you.

You can stay where you are, in heart of compassion. Or you can crack your heart open just a tiny bit more. It's up to you.

251

IF YOU CRACK YOUR HEART OPEN into Oneness, you're going to have to leave things behind. It's a joyous stepping into a new consciousness. But not everyone will be able to go there with you.

What skin are you ready to shed? What beliefs are you ready to let go of?

252

IF YOU ARE IN THE MIDST OF spiritual awakening, you may feel as though you walk around the earth with your skin peeled back, with your skin raw to everything. You may take everything in: energy, emotion, and vibration. This is a part of what opening feels like.

When things feel too much, what do you do? Do you protect yourself? Do you hide away? What if, just for today, you merged with it all?

253

YOU HAVE THIS IDEA OF PROTECTION, of protecting yourself with energy. There is no protection! As one of One, this is impossible. All things vibrate, all things merge, all energy is all energy. This idea keeps you in fear.

You are not separate. Walk around with that thought today.

254

THE SHAMANIC DRUGS, THE ECSTATIC DRUGS, the recreational drugs, the physician-prescribed drugs, the mood-altering drugs, the alcohol—all these substances are used in hopes the body will experience Oneness. These are real experiences! Expansion can be possible! But it is easier on your physical container if you experience this with the mind.

Do you take drugs? Can you feel the way you feel with drugs, on your own? Why not?

255

WHEN YOU APPLY THE IDEA OF ONENESS to all aspects of your life: relationships, healthy, money, and material things, you begin to shift your dreams. The idea of amassing *things* loses its luster as the idea of *being* becomes more important than having.

In this temporal life what do you need to have, own, and amass? Are you sure?

256

IN THE STATE OF ONENESS the idea of security, safety, protection, and stability also drops away. Everything changes. Happiness is an internal state, not based on externals. It is hard to see this until you are there.

What makes you feel secure: Money? Material things? Marriage? Children? What are you banking on for your future? Would you exist if this went away?

257

PEOPLE WHO'VE LOST EVERYTHING walk around as though dazed for a while. They see something we don't see: that they still exist without all the things that once defined them.

What defines you? Who are you? Make a list, then look at it from the perspective of Oneness.

258

WE'RE SPECIFIC, YES. We have characteristics, we have gifts, we have flaws and foibles. But at our essence we are the same—not just with each other, but with every energy in the Universe.

What is specific about you? What are the gifts you brought into your human life this time around? Are you using them?

259

YOUR GIFTS LEAD YOU TO YOUR LIFE'S WORK. This is why you have these specific, unique gifts. The one who can work with energy becomes a healer. The one who can hear the guides, angels, and ascended beings becomes a teacher. The one who sees visions becomes a leader. And so forth, and so on.

Your gifts are holy. Your gifts are mundane. Write a list of your gifts. How can you make use of these?

260

IN THE HEART OF CONNECTION, where spiritual awakening begins, where consciousness begins, we often speak of "entering a new life." It is true. When consciousness arrives you enter life on the spiritual plane,

Can you be spiritual while living an earth life? Do you need to go to the mountaintop? Or can you live this way from where you are now?

261

CONSCIOUSNESS; IT DOESN'T MEAN you walk around every moment talking to angels, seeing energy fields, and existing in a state of nirvanic meditation. It just means you're wide awake. You've dropped the illusions.

You will have an opportunity to be fully present today. Be ready.

262

CONSCIOUSNESS DOESN'T MEAN life without pain. It means you slide into pain, but you don't stay there. You quickly rise from pain to compassion, and then to connection. It's effortless to become One in any situation.

Today, when you feel pain, make the progression immediately: pain to compassion to connection. Notice you can do this about a million times faster than you could at the beginning of the year.

263

PAIN IS NO LONGER SOMETHING to be feared! Do you see this? How quickly now you may transmute these emotional states, by diving in and opening the heart through the progression: pain, compassion, connection.

Practice this! Choose a subject that still causes you pain. Dive into heart of pain. Now, keep progressively opening.

264

WHEN YOU REACH HEART OF CONNECTION, when you understand yourself as One, pain can no longer hold you. Fear can't hold you. You're vibrating at a level above these, and you can hold this vibration. You've shifted from numbness to consciousness.

If you're feeling conscious, congratulations! If you're not sure, open further. Let everything drop away that is not One.

265

YOU DON'T NEED TO FOLLOW a spiritual practice to become one with One. You don't have to light incense, do asanas, make a pilgrimage, or go on a vision quest. These are just decorations, accessories, and adornments.

In your life, what do you call spiritual practice that is really just another attachment?

266

WHEN YOU ARE IN THE HEART OF CONNECTION, consciousness shifts. You find you can lock into the hum of the Universe at any time, at any place. There is no time you can't do this.

Feel the hum of the Universe around you right now. You may perceive this as a tingling of the air on your skin, a quickening in your brain, or an expansion in your heart. Lock into this hum.

267

CONSCIOUSNESS SHIFTS. IT HAPPENS in an instant. There is no time this can't happen to you, or to anyone. If you are awake you may move into consciousness as frequently as you like; each time you slip into the dream you may move into the awake state again.

We are constantly sliding from state to state. When you feel yourself getting numb, shutting down, or contracting, simply expand your heart.

268

HOW DO OTHER, NON-HUMAN BEINGS attain consciousness? Is this the same level humans have? Do other etheric entities have higher levels of consciousness? Is Oneness the highest vibration we can feel? Is love?

Consider these ideas as you move through your day.

269

BEING CONSCIOUS IS MORE THAN JUST ABOUT "being here now." It's about being here now and seeing the dream. Seeing the dream, dreaming the dreaming, being in the dream, and knowing they're all the same.

What is the dream, to you? What's real? Is there a difference, really?

270

NOTHING MATTERS. EVERYTHING MATTERS. Somewhere between the two is a great place to live your life.

What is one thing you would do today if nothing mattered? If everything mattered?

271

WHEN IT GETS DOWN TO IT, all the philosophy in the world means nothing. What's important is your own experience—what you believe.

What makes sense to you today? What's important? What else?

272

YOU CAN GO SO FAR OUT ON A SPIRITUAL LEDGE, in full understanding of the dream, that you forget we're also earth beings. We walk on dirt. We procreate through our bodies. We have messy emotions. All of this happens simultaneously. This is our experience.

What's messy in your life?

273

It's hard to understand everything all at once. The human mind can't grasp it. We have a zoom lens that goes from huge to minuscule. The whole picture, from sacred to mundane, is too much to grasp at once. This is okay.

Pick one mundane thing in your life and make it sacred, such as doing the dishes in a state of grace. Pick one sacred thing and make in mundane, such as praying as you mow the lawn.

274

Sacred and mundane are not actually two states. Life is all one state, everything happening at all levels and layers, in all dimensions, simultaneously, beyond time. It's all infinite states.

Try to grasp it for five seconds. Just open yourself and feel it. Then go about your day.

275

When you reach this level of consciousness you understand we are dreaming the dream, and the dream arrives to us as "real." This means you may begin to create your dream, should you choose. In fact, you already have.

Are you living your dream life? Actually, you are. Do you like it? What's a better dream?

276

YOU DON'T NEED TO LEARN how to manifest, attract, or create. You've been doing it your whole life. But maybe you need to dream bigger dreams.

What is your absolutely biggest dream? What if you could live this dream?

277

IT ISN'T IMPORTANT WHETHER YOU LIVE a "big" life, or a "small" life. The amount of pleasure, joy, bliss, connection, passion, interest, and fascination in your life cannot be measured by society's standards.

Are you enjoying your experience? As you move through your day today, notice what's enjoyable.

278

CONSCIOUSNESS, THE UNDERSTANDING OF YOURSELF as one with One, brings a deep understanding of other people, situations, the past, the present, and energy. We often call this psychic understanding, or intuition.

Today, try to do a psychic reading on every person you meet. Don't tell them what you're doing. Just try it and see what happens.

279

INTUITION IS MERELY A MATTER OF locking into the hum, of locking into collective soul of One. Each of us has this ability when we are in heart of connection.

Do you consider yourself intuitive? Do you think everyone is, or can be? How does this change how you look at ideas like "thoughts" or "destiny?"

280

WHEN YOU'RE ONE, AND YOU UNDERSTAND everyone else is also One, it's easy to think intuitively. You're not separate—so you have access to the same information, which is collective soul.

What intuitive moments have you had in your life? Recently, have you had more of these moments?

281

IS COLLECTIVE SOUL THE SAME AS GROUP THOUGHT? No. Group thought lives in the lower vibrations of fear, anger, and rage. Collective soul is group thought raised to the highest vibration, the vibration of Oneness. It is also more than human.

Let your mind meander today, to the idea of collective soul. What information do you think is contained in the Universe?

282

COLLECTIVE SOUL IS CALLED DIFFERENT THINGS: God, One, All, Divine, Source, and Universe are some of these terms. Akashic Records, Matrix, and unified field are others. There are many terms for One.

Close your eyes and imagine a large, ancient book filled with all the information about your life you could ever need. Imagine this book also contains all your past lives and all your future lives . What does this book say?

283

MANY OTHER ENTITIES EXIST in this Universe: aliens, who are merely beings from other planets, plus etheric entities, such as angels, guides, the ascended, and the departed—a countless multitude. These are also part of collective soul. These are also sentient beings.

How do you feel, thinking about aliens? How do you feel, thinking about angels?

284

WE ARE CONTINUALLY GUIDED BY other etheric beings. You may accept this idea as actual beings, as your subconscious, or as your higher self. Words and labels don't matter. The Divine guidance is still there.

Do you believe angels guide you, or do you believe you're guided by your higher, Divine self? Does it matter which theory is right?

285

ENTITIES, INCLUDING THE DEPARTED, continually pass in and out of the "veil" that separates this reality from other realities. All is reality. Or, it's all a dream, whichever term you like to use. No separation here, either.

Would it bother you to see or communicate with the departed? Would this change your view of death?

286

THE PERSON WHO DIES AMID GRIEF will be welcomed again with much joy during reincarnation. Pain turns into bliss, in a continual cycle.

What do you believe happens when you die?

287

WHEN SOMEONE DIES, WE ARE REMINDED this is also our journey. When someone is born, we are reminded of whence we came. Both passages are mysteries. The heart holds their only meaning.

The cycle is birth, death, birth, death. Just notice this cycle in your life today in all the ways it shows up.

288

THE PAIN OF LOSING SOMEONE WE LOVE can seem beyond endurance. We think, in this moment, that death has taken them away forever. And yet, in the soul's time this is not true.

If you could communicate with a departed loved one, would this be healing for you? Ask for this to happen if you are ready.

289

THE DEPARTED ARE GONE FROM THIS REALITY, from this Now. But they are not gone. They continue into new lives, new experiences. We will do this too, one day.

Do you believe in reincarnation? In past lives? In life after death? What do you think happens?

290

PERHAPS YOU HAVE HAD VISIONS of yourself in other times; you are unrecognizable to yourself, and yet you also understand clearly that this is you. These may be past lives or they may be concurrent realities.

What do your dreams and visions show you about who you have been in other lifetimes? Don't censor; write down the first thing that comes to mind.

291

IF WE WEREN'T BORN, IF WE DIDN'T DIE, there would be no "container" for this particular human lifetime. The finite nature of our lives is what makes them extraordinary.

What else do you want to experience in the time you have left?

292

WE DON'T FEAR DEATH; we fear the end of this lifetime. The souls we have met, the great feast of experiences we have enjoyed; these have challenged us, taught us, and filled us. This particular lifetime is overwhelmingly beautiful.

How is it a gift to be human? Write down ten ways.

293

THE OTHER ENTITIES THAT CROSS PATH in our layers and levels of consciousness don't have the human experience. They see all past, all future, and all life as energetic. They see the contraction and expansion of energy, beyond particular experience.

If you were an entity: a saint, an angel, a guide, an ascended—what view would you take of the human experience?

294

OUR GUIDES AND ANGELS ALWAYS BRING US Divine love, because we forget to hold this vibration. They hold this vibration all the time, whereas our own vibration is constantly changing, like a wave that recedes and then forms again.

If you were a guide or angel, what would you tell a human being? What would you tell yourself?

295

THOSE WHO ARE EMBARRASSED or don't like the terms guides, angels, or entities, can use the idea of their higher selves, Divine self, or another idea that is less personal. The guides don't care.

Do you think angels exist? What about guides? Why or why not?

296

GUIDE AND ANGELS ARE ENERGETIC ENTITIES. They don't look as they appear to us; they create this imagery so we can more easily relate to them. Their vibration is much higher than we can see.

Do you see or sense entities? Can you feel a shift in vibration where you are even now, reading this? Take a moment and see what you feel.

297

WE BEST UNDERSTAND WHAT IS FAMILIAR. We best understand what we already know a little about. Thus, an angel shows up with wings and robes because this is what we accept, this is the story we've been told for generations. But the costume itself isn't real.

If you could have a guide or angel appear to you, how would this entity look? What personality would he or she have? Meditate today and see who shows up.

298

ANGELS AND GUIDES WORK EFFORTLESSLY in the energy stream of electronica. It is the simplest thing for them to stall a car when you should not be driving. It is the simplest thing for them to send a message to you on the radio.

When you get in your car today, notice what song is on the radio. If you don't have a car, notice the first song you hear. What does this song mean to you?

299

WE OFTEN SEE OUR ANGELS AND GUIDES clearly when we are children, but as we grow older we forget to see them. And yet, it is easy to see into these other layers and levels of consciousness. Going there again is no big deal.

Close your eyes and ask the Universe to reveal the presence of angels or guides to you. Don't try to "see," just sense the presence. Notice if an entity is with you and if this entity seems familiar.

300

THE "DARK" ENERGIES ARE LOWER VIBRATION. When you're in high vibration you don't even see them or notice them. They aren't even in your reality. Your entire experience in this world is determined by your vibration and consciousness. In other words, how much your heart is open through pain, compassion, and connection.

Where is your heart today? If you are in low vibration, hovering near pain, remember that you can transmute this now: move effortlessly through pain, into compassion and connection.

301

YOUR ABILITY TO TRANSMUTE YOUR EMOTIONS: to feel pain fully and then transmute this into compassion, into connection—this transforms your life. You are now able to move effortlessly from low vibration to high vibration, using these sequential, consecutive passages of the heart.

As an experiment today, see how quickly you can move through the three passages: pain to compassion to connection. What differences do you notice each time you do this?

302

BEING ABLE TO MOVE INTO HEART OF CONNECTION, into beginning of consciousness and awakening, doesn't mean you won't feel pain again. It just means you'll have a way to move forward when you do feel pain.

Do you expect your life to be only "good?" Have you noticed that great learning comes from experiencing what is not ideal?

303

LIKE A WAVE, LIFE SWELLS FORWARD and recedes. It's always in a constant cycle of moving forward, receding backward. We like to think we're making progress in the "forward" phase. And yet, the negative space—the gathering phase—this is where we collect our strength.

Does something always need to be happening in your life? Do you always feel you should be moving forward? How do you feel if you do nothing, if you just rest?

304

WHEN YOU ARE IN THE HEART OF CONNECTION you have the ability to co-create with the Universe. The trouble is, what to ask for, what to manifest? In truth, you need ask for nothing. All you require for soul growth is already provided.

When you manifest, what do you ask for? Today, consider not manifesting, not attracting anything at all. And then see what happens.

305

WHEN YOU UNDERSTAND HOW TO "ATTRACT," creating your earth life is simple. You simply request what you'd like, you put your attention there—and this thing arrives. And yet, this is just one way to live. If you were to choose to not consciously "attract," you would attract anyway.

How effective are you at "attracting?" Do you feel frustration when you try to "attract," and nothing happens? What if the reason for things not happening had nothing to do with you?

306

WHEN YOU CREATE WITH THE ENERGY OF INTENTION, with your mind, energy is created—it is manifested for you. However, it is not possible to manifest from the lower vibration of pain, fear, and anger. It is not even possible to manifest from compassion. You must move into heart of connection. Oneness is the required vibration.

Today, think of what you would like to create. Then meditate on Oneness; enter the heart of connection. Don't manifest; just hold the vibration. Just allow the vibration to lead you.

307

WHAT SHOULD YOU MANIFEST? Nothing? Everything? In truth, it's all the same. Whatever you request from the Universe will show up in its time, and this particular confluence will assist you in your soul growth.

Stop worrying about doing it right. Just stop worrying. Hold heart of connection and understand yourself as one of One today. That's enough.

308

THE "LAW OF ATTRACTION" STATES that you attract what you are. But you are all parts: divine and mundane, sacred and profane, particulate and One. In other words, the Universe attracts itself, in all the ways it is itself.

If you attract what you are, what are you? What else? What else? You attract all these things in order to integrate fully.

309

YOU CAN MANIFEST A MANSION with your intention; you can manifest financial ruin. Again, what you manifest is not as important as why. The Universe always chooses your highest possibility: in other words, you get what you need for soul growth.

Take a look at what you want, today. Make a list! Now, look at this list from the perspective of soul growth. See if this changes what you want.

310

THERE WILL ALWAYS BE ANOTHER DESIRE, another attraction, another distraction. To detach from the need to manifest, attract, and control will provide a new kind of freedom. When you approach each day as Divine experience—this creates peace, enjoyment, and fulfillment.

Forget what you are trying to create today. Instead, ask yourself: "What would I enjoy the most in this hour? In the next three hours? Later still, in this day?

311

WE THINK WE ARE ONLY CREATING when we're awake, but this is not true. The times of sleep and dreams, the times when we are not conscious in the world—we are exquisitely conscious as souls during this dream state.

What dreams did you have last night? If you cannot remember your dreams, close your eyes and allow a new dream to fill your mind. What is it?

312

OUR DREAMS DON'T ARRIVE SIMPLY to inform us. Instead, they *are* us: our dream state is as important and real as the waking state. They aren't separate. They both make up our selves, our lives.

How did you sleep last night? Do you notice, as we speak of dreams, that your dreams are becoming more active, more clear, and you are remembering them more vividly?

313

OUR DREAMS ARE A STATE OF CONSCIOUSNESS beyond the consciousness we are able to hold in waking life. In other words, we are more conscious, more in the realm of soul when we are in our dreams then when we are awake.

What do your dreams tell you about your soul? If you are not sure, close your eyes and allow this story to come to you.

314

THE SLEEPING DREAM AND THE WAKING DREAM are all one dream. There is no separation between the layers and levels of the Universe. When you understand yourself as one of One, this becomes clear.

What happens to you when you sleep? Where do you go? Do you see that you are part of the Universe, no matter what state you are in?

315

OUR DREAMS DON'T JUST INFORM US. They are us. There is no separation between the waking state, the dreaming state, and any other state such as past, future, life, and death. These are separations we draw: they do not, in fact, exist.

Consider if you are more you when you are in the waking state or in the dreaming state. Consider which is more "real." Think about this today.

316

IF ALL LIFE IS A DREAM, DOES IT MATTER? It does matter. The human experience is specific and special; it allows the soul to achieve growth that cannot happen when the soul is not attached to a body. You are perhaps more divine because you have the human experience. This opens you.

If you were an untethered entity, what do you think this would be like? Do you think you have been untethered before: in a past life, in a life between lives, or during other aspects of your soul's journey?

317

WHEN YOU BEGIN TO SEE ENTITIES, the departed, you notice how crowded this world is. Each room, space, and area is crowded with energies: most with souls, others simply with thought forms. The crowding may surprise you—the amount of light generated by so many entities, at so many layers and levels, everywhere, all the time.

Do you feel the presence of entities where you are? Take a moment now and see if you can feel a shimmering on your shoulder or a density in the room. This is not the first time you have noticed.

318

YOU CAN COMMUNICATE WITH ENTITIES; you can communicate with saints, the holy ones, and you can communicate with the departed. The line of separation is illusion. It can be crossed safely when you are working in energy of the Divine.

When you choose higher vibration, you will always travel to the place of highest vibration. This is where you want to go. Consider now if any part of you seeks the dark. Ask if you still need this, or if you are done with it.

319

THOSE WHO SEEK THE DARK DO SO to be in pain. They believe it is easier to stay there; but it is not. If you are in pain, if you are still moving from pain into compassion, take a look at this now.

Pain is dark. Love is light. Light is the place you are ultimately headed. Ask your heart if it is ready to make this transition.

320

IT IS POSSIBLE TO GO INTO HEART OF LOVE without having made the full progression from pain, but it is not possible to stay there if you have not done the progression. However, the more times you enter love and the more times you hold this feeling of highest vibration, the easier it will be to move into this state.

Go now, into love. Close your eyes and go into a state of absolute bliss, love, nirvana, joy, and transcendence. You can do this effortlessly! Bathe yourself in it, imbue yourself! Remember this feeling.

321

EVERY TIME YOU EXIST IN LOVE you make it easier to get there again. This is why it is so useful to meditate, pray, and have direct connection with the Divine. The connection is personal, not something you can do any other way. No one can meditate for you or pray for you.

When do you meditate? When do you pray? This is the path to love.

322

THIS BLISSFUL FEELING YOU GET when you enter heart of love? This is what the Universe is. It is what you are. There is no difference.

Why don't you always feel the pure bliss and joy of the heart of love? Would you like to feel it more? What aspects do you have to change before this can begin to happen?

323

GO INTO MEDITATION AND ENTER BLISS. Then heal yourself with this Divine love and light. Now go back into your earth life and begin cracking your heart open through the four passages: pain, compassion, and connection. Every time you drop into low vibration, do this process again.

Enter bliss today, three times. Just notice how the vibration feels. See how quickly you can go into this state.

324

WHEN YOU UNDERSTAND THE STEPS to take, how to move consecutively toward heart's expansion, your life begins to transform. You become conscious, you live in high vibration, and you are able at any time to move from low to high vibration.

Hold a state of love. Now think of something that bothers you. Immediately move through the passages: pain, compassion, and connection until you reach love again. Notice how easy this is becoming for you.

325

YOU BECOME CONSCIOUS when you reach heart of connection. You become transcendent when you reach heart of love. This is where the saints, the masters, and the ascended live.

Put up the image of a cup in your mind and imagine this cup contains love. What percentage of your cup is full today—one third, one half, over flowing? Do this a few times today and notice what happens.

326

THE HEART OF LOVE ISN'T ABOUT LOVING a specific person. It's about loving all specific people, as One. You begin to open your heart when you love one person: a romantic partner, a child. But when you open your heart further into love, there is room for more than one.

Write a list of every single person you love. Don't stop until you absolutely can't think of any more.

327

PAIN IS THE HARDEST PASSAGE, then compassion. By the time you have moved into connection, into realizing yourself as one of One, moving into heart of love is the easiest, simplest step. It's a simple sigh, a breath, and you have shifted into transcendence, bliss, and joy.

Today, see yourself as one of One. Just look at everything around you and know this. Then one deep breath—and you have opened into love. Ahhhh.

328

WHAT DOES UNDERSTANDING ONESELF as one of One look like? All is revealed as particulate energy; all particulate swirling energy in the Universe that is you, he, she, rock, table, spoon. All particulate swirling energy is swirling infinitely, always, without end.

Close your eyes halfway and begin to see what is particulate. To see better still, close your eyes and allow this idea of particulate energy to swirl in your mind, in all dimensions.

329

PARTICULATE ENERGY DOES NOT ONLY include matter. It also extends to time, space, other dimensions, realms, frequencies and vibrations you don't have names for. Understand: this is also One.

How do you think time works? What about space? Close your eyes and let your mind wander to these concepts. See if you are informed in a new way.

330

WHEN YOU UNDERSTAND EVERYTHING as One, all dimensions, then you can easily move in the layers and levels of these dimensions. This ability begins when you become conscious; when you open to heart of connection. In this state you are able to understand energy and to access collective soul.

How do you think about energy? About collective soul? Today, allow yourself to be informed in a new way, by a message that comes into your life.

331

COLLECTIVE SOUL HAS MANY NAMES: Universe, energy, source, Akashic records, unified field, or matrix. Oneness is yet another term. When you open into the heart of connection, into Oneness, you tap into collective soul. Your vibration raises, your consciousness expands, and this is the natural, normal next step.

Go into heart of connection. Now allow yourself to hear the whisperings of collective soul. You have heard this many, many times. Now hear it with intention.

332

IN ORDER TO WORK WITH ENERGY and intuition, you needn't have complete understanding of how things work. You just have to trust that the process—the expansion of the heart that leads to conscious awakening—works. That's the only technique you need.

Think about all the things you've heard about intuition, energy, awakening, and so forth. Now write down what you believe.

333

WHEN YOU ARE IN HEART OF CONNECTION you exist as One. In this way it is effortless for you to connect into collective soul, unified field, all the names for One. And in this way it is effortless for you to intuitively see into the future and into the past.

At this time of your heart's opening, of your consciousness shift, how do you use your intuition? How do you access it?

334

WHEN YOU OPEN TO HEART OF CONNECTION you also open to realms of guides, angels, ascended masters, holy ones, saints and other beings who exist in this vibration. These begins or entities are always there; but until you open to heart of connection you will rarely see them.

Do you communicate with Divine entities? Do you want to? If you would like to begin this journey and open into heart of connection, understand yourself as One and simply ask for this to begin for you.

335

YOU WILL FIND IT HARD TO COMMUNICATE with God/Divine/One/All in a specific way. The energy is complicated and overwhelming—so big that language and imagery isn't possible. This is where the guides, angels, and so forth come in: their energy is higher than ours, so they are able to act as translators, go-betweens, and decoders for us.

When you enter a state where you are receiving much Universal information all at once, ask for a guide to arrive who will help you understand the meaning more clearly. Simply ask in your mind for this to happen.

336

SOMETIMES YOU WILL RECEIVE A "DOWNLOAD" of information from the Universe, all at once. This may come in dreams, in a waking state, in trance state, or at any time. You suddenly become aware of information coming into your thoughts in a concentrated, fast way. This will shift you into further vibration and understanding.

You may ask for a download at any time. Simply close your eyes, enter heart of connection, and ask for a download to begin. You may feel a tingling or have a sense of rushing energy when this happens.

337

WHAT HAPPENS WHEN YOU ARE EXISTING in heart of connection and come across lower vibrations: people, places, or objects? In most cases, you will raise the vibration of whoever, and whatever, you've encountered. If you find this is difficult, simply request that a guide will come to help you.

Are people you are close to at a lower vibration? When? Why? Does this affect you, or not?

338

IT ISN'T YOUR JOB TO FIX PEOPLE. It is your delight to heal them, if they ask you. But if nothing is asked of you, simply continue to vibrate at the highest level you can manage.

When you vibrate higher than others, don't go to their level. Just vibrate where you vibrate and allow this to permeate the relationship, the situation, and the events. Just be as you are, in light.

339

WHEN HEART OF CONNECTION SHIFTS to heart of love, this is the easiest step. It's a natural expansion. With this shift in vibration, consciousness also deepens. Hold space in heart of love long enough, and you become transcendent.

Recall what transcendence feels like: how the body feels, the heart, the mind, and the soul. Think about this completely and fully. Notice if you have gone there in this remembering.

340

IN YOUR WHOLE LIFE, nothing is more important than learning how to open into heart of love. This is your soul's journey; the way in which we experience soul growth through the human heart.

Think of your ambitions, your must dos, your schedules. Measure these against your soul's journey into heart of love. What arrives to you?

341

DON'T WORRY IF YOU AREN'T ABLE to stay in heart of love easily yet. To enter this vibrational state takes practice: a continual consecutive opening of the heart through pain, compassion, and connection, every time this is needed. Enough practice, and love becomes your new state.

How do you think you would feel if you were able to stay in heart of love for ten minutes today? How about for an hour, a full day, or a week? Do you think this is possible for a human? Is it possible for you?

342

THE GREAT MASTERS, THE SAINTS and holy ones, were able to exist in heart of love for long periods of time. Eventually, at some point, they simply transcended their human vibration into a higher vibration still. Heart of love is the point of transcendence.

What masters or holy ones do you align with? Picture these beings in your mind and imagine their hearts of love.

343

IT IS NOT EVERYONE'S PATH to become a transcendent being, to lift off entirely from earth life. Some of you will reach heart of pain and find it hard to go further. Some of you will reach heart of compassion. If you are able to reach heart of connection, you will find it easy to reach heart of love. You may not be able to stay there in all moments of your life; but you will have tasted this bliss, the nectar of love.

Do you want to experience heart of love? Ask now, and it is yours.

344

WHEN YOU HAVE MOMENTS of transcendence, time seems to shift gears: an hour passes in a minute, a minute takes hours. Every time you notice time shifting, realize that you are in a state of trance, nirvana, and bliss that is heart of love.

When was the last time you noticed time shifting? Do you notice it now, as the world expands in consciousness? Watch today for this phenomenon.

345

WHAT HOPES DO YOU HAVE for the world's transcendence? These will all come to fruition. Just as the guides, the angels, the ascended, and the saints and holy ones made this transition, so too will humans. Time is not so long as it seems.

How many people do you know who have gained consciousness and become spiritually awake in the last few years? Write down their names now. Rejoice in them, the gift of these souls to your life!

346

AFTER A WHILE, AFTER YOU HAVE EXISTED in heart of love enough times, your life profoundly changes. Your perspective changes entirely; what was "bad" no longer looks bad. What was "good" no longer looks good. You lose attachment to ideas or concepts and instead just hold love in your own heart.

How has your view shifted during this year of study? Write down five worries, angers, or other "negative" thoughts you used to have, and how they have shifted or transformed.

347

WHEN YOUR PERSPECTIVE SHIFTS, when you become transformed and transmuted by your experience in heart of love, the outside aspects of your life also change. This is much more than "law of attraction," or "manifesting." This is much beyond "integration" or "shadow." You have moved beyond all of this.

What did you believe before, when you started this course? What do you believe now? Try to write it in five sentences. Then in just one. Is there a way to say it in words?

348

GOD, GOD, GOD: UNIVERSE/ONE/DIVINE/SOURCE/ALL. Everything gets to be just this: you, the world that surrounds you, the people and beings you meet, all time and space. You exist in love, you exist in pure flow. Nothing else matters.

How is your life in flow today? How has your life shifted to flow during this year?

349

WHEN YOU EXIST IN HEART OF LOVE, flow is the only way you can live. When you exist in flow, you exist in effortless enjoyment, effortless integration, effortless rapture of all that is. You are like a Sufi swirling in bliss, a yogi meditating, a saint in trance—but you exist this way all the time, even as you go about your regular day.

It's grace, this way of being. What are your acts of grace, today? When will you be in flow?

350

IN HEART OF LOVE, THE EXPANSION is so great it can be overwhelming at first. But delve into this Divine infusion, this Divine healing, this Divine expansion often enough and it becomes your new norm, your baseline where you most often live.

Write of the time when you first experienced this expansion: a time of spiritual awakening. Write of how it is to live now, awake.

351

YOU MAY REACH HEART OF LOVE by making direct connection with the Divine. How is your meditation practice? Do you dance? Are you in nature? Are you connecting authentically and deeply with others? All these open heart of love.

Today, what has your practice been? How have you moved from connection to love?

352

ONCE YOU ENTER HEART OF LOVE you see that desires are fleeting, transitory, not of importance to you. When you know yourself as One and then you expand further, the mundane aspects disappear. And yet, you must integrate these states: Divine and human. Such is the journey of soul growth.

How are you integrating your Divine and human selves? What problems do you still have in this integration?

353

IT'S EASY TO SIT ON THE MOUNTAIN TOP IN HEART OF LOVE. It's hard to come back down to the foothills of your mundane life, and still hold bliss. This is the journey of soul growth! This is the journey of being human!

When you find yourself descending into heart of pain, how do you approach this now? Do you remember to begin the expansion through pain, compassion, connection? If this is hard for you, take a look at why.

354

PERFECTION IS NOT THE KEY. Living continually in heart of love is not the point. However, the ability to see that you are both Divine and mundane, and to have a method of shifting vibration from low to high states—this will entirely change your life.

Are you ready to give up perfection, being "good," and being a spiritual over achiever? Are you ready to be your full human and Divine self?

355

YOU ARE NOT MEANT TO BE "PERFECT." It is of no importance that you hold heart of love at all times. Soul growth is a journey of this lifetime, last live time, and next life time. Hold heart of love as you can. This is entirely enough.

How does it feel that you do not need to be perfect? How does it feel to know that you have plenty of time as an infinite Divine being?

356

THE DIVINE/UNIVERSE/GOD/ONE/ALL ... you'll never understand it. As a human, there are only glimpses of ascendant grace, of transmutation. This is plenty. One drop of Divine infusion contains all the healing, all the transcendence you will ever require.

Today, right now, hold connection with Divine/Universe/God/One/All. Expand beyond all of your hearts, through all the passages and into love. Bask in this Divine energy, this infusion, this healing, this grace.

357

IF YOU ARE HAVING A DIRECT CONNECTION with the Divine you will find it hard to come back down and live in heart of pain. In fact, this soon becomes impossible. The more you are infused, the more transformed you become.

Do you notice how you feel differently about people in your life now? Do you notice how the old pain, the old complaints, the old anger has dissipated? Write about the relationships that have transformed in this year.

358

PRACTICES SUCH AS MEDITATION, yoga, prayer, and such are meant to bring you to consciousness, to help you experience direct connection with the Divine. Once you have experienced this, the practice is no longer needed. You know how to get there without the tool.

Consider your practices. Do any seem flat to you, as if you have moved beyond them? Consider if you need them still.

359

CONSCIOUSNESS IS A GREAT SHIFTING; you move into a new place, and those in your life may or may not move with you. The Universe is always in a state of change. It may be difficult to understand that things shift and relationships change, yet this is also part of the earth experience.

What relationships have shifted for you during this past year? Hold these now in heart of love.

360

ATTAINING HEART OF LOVE DOES NOT MEAN your earth life will from this point on be perfect bliss and nirvana. It just means that at any time you have a method of direct connection with the highest vibrational energy, which is love. This energy transforms every situation, every aspect, and every understanding.

Consider a moment in your day today that was less than ideal. Now, look at this moment from heart of love. How does holding this vibration reframe the moment?

361

CONSIDER YOUR LIFE ONE YEAR AGO: the ups and downs, the "mistakes," the "failures" the grief, the losses. Understand that in the future you will also experience these. However, your perception will be different because you are now awake.

Make a timeline of your life from birth to last year, noting important events or changes. Use this timeline to revisit your life to this point. Now, make a timeline from last year to now. Notice where you have changed.

362

WHEN YOU UNDERSTAND HOW TO EXPAND your heart through the four passages: when you have had Divine infusion so your consciousness has changed, you have arrived to a new way of living. You can always reach love by moving through the four passages. This sets you free.

Think of today and notice when you were awake and when asleep. Recall if you chose to move through the four passages at any time, or if you now do this expansion automatically.

363

YOUR JOURNEY OF SOUL GROWTH does not end in this lifetime, or the next lifetime, or the next. Understand this. Enjoy your time here.

Today, spend your day in full expansion into heart of love. Enjoy this life.

364

EVERY TIME YOU SENSE PAIN, you have a choice. To stay in pain. Or to expand the heart into love, one passage at a time.

Your life is yours to create. In this lifetime, you will be asked to make this choice—from pain into love—in every minute, in every second. You can only choose, in each separate experience of Now. How do you choose, in this moment?

365

WHEREVER YOU ARE, IS PERFECT. Simply know where you are, look at it, illuminate it. Heart of love arrives, whenever you are in connection with the Divine.

If your only purpose in life was your presence, how would you choose to live? In pain? In compassion? In connection? In love?

ABOUT THE AUTHOR

Spiritual teacher and intuitive Sara Wiseman is the author of

* *Becoming Your Best Self: The Guide to Clarity, Inspiration and Joy,*
* *Writing the Divine: How to Use Channeling for Soul Growth & Healing,*
* *Your Psychic Child: How to Raise Intuitive & Spiritually Gifted Kids of All Ages,* and
* *The Miracle of Gratitude: 108 Ways to Live in Joy and Grace.*

She hosts the CBS New Sky radio show *Ask Sara*, is a top contributor to DailyOM, and has released four healing CDs with her band Martyrs of Sound. She works privately with clients worldwide.

For more information, please visit **www.sarawiseman.com**

AUDIO SUPPORT

For this book, Sara Wiseman has created *The Four Passages of the Heart* audio course, a series of four guided meditations accompanied by healing music from her award-winning band Martyrs of Sound. This audio course is ideal for talking you deeper into the experience of opening your heart into the four passages of consciousness.

Sara Wiseman also offers a variety of audio courses to complement her teachings and books, as well as free podcasts from her popular CBS New Sky radio show *Ask Sara*.

For complete information on audio courses and podcasts, visit **www.sarawiseman.com**

Books by Sara Wiseman

BECOMING YOUR BEST SELF
The Guide to Clarity, Inspiration and Joy

What if you could receive Divine guidance at any time? What if you could clearly see your highest potential? What if you could heal the past, live in the present, and manifest your dreams in the future? In this delightfully inspiring books, Sara Wiseman teaches you how to establish a direct connection with the Divine that will raise your vibration, heal your heart, allow instant access to Universal information, and transform your life in the process.

Through step-by-step exercises you will learn a variety of life-changing skills—from attracting a soul mate to healing relationships to communicating with Divine guides and loved ones in spirit. Throughout, Wiseman shares simple yet profound messages that open the path to a new level of consciousness and to your own spiritual awakening.

978-0-7387-2794-3, 264 pp., 6 x 9
$16.95

YOUR PSYCHIC CHILD

How to Raise Intuitive & Spiritually Gifted Kids of All Ages

Want to take an active role in your child's psychic and spiritual development? This indispensable guide helps parents understand and nurture their uniquely gifted children.

Learn about the psychic awakening process and the talents that emerge with each age, from toddler to teen. Discover how to gently encourage your children to explore and develop their strengths in clairvoyance, energy healing and mediumship, and teach them how to connect with the Divine. Anchored in down-to-earth parental wisdom and alive with personal anecdotes, *Your Psychic Child* is an essential resource for parents who recognize their child's psychic and spiritual potential.

978-0-7387-2061-6, 312 pp., 6 x 9
$17.95

WRITING THE DIVINE

How to Use Channeling for Soul Growth & Healing

This amazing book shows you that learning channeling and channeled writing isn't just for gurus and psychics—it's as easy as closing your eyes and picking up your pen! In part one, Sara Wiseman shares clear, simple directions for divine receiving, how to use a journal for spiritual growth, and how to manifest in writing.

Part two invites you to experience directly the transformative power of The 33 Lessons, an inspiring collection of Divine lessons received by Wiseman, on love, life and spiritual awakening in this world.

978-0-7387-1581-0, 312 pp., 6 x 9
$16.95

MUSIC BY MARTYRS OF SOUND

Sara Wiseman and Dr. Steve Koc create award-winning music with their band Martyrs of Sound. This music is ideal for meditation, prayer, yoga, massage, relaxation, insomnia, and healing, and is widely played on international airwaves.

Their albums include:

Mantra Chill: Serene, luminous and healing mantra.
Uncoiled: Tribal dance trance for chakra opening from root to crown.
Songs for Loving & Dying: Tantric rock with a spiritual groove.
Radhe's Dream: Song of the Beloved, as expressed in healing mantra.

Listen and download at **www.martyrsofsound.com**

Made in the USA
Middletown, DE
27 February 2019